ROY FULLER

COLLECTED POEMS

Also by Roy Fuller

*

ROY FULLER

Broadbent

11

, 1912–

COLLECTED POEMS
1936–1961

ANDRE DEUTSCH

FIRST PUBLISHED 1962 BY
ANDRE DEUTSCH LIMITED
105 GREAT RUSSELL STREET
LONDON WC I
COPYRIGHT © 1962 BY ROY FULLER
ALL RIGHTS RESERVED
PRINTED IN GREAT BRITAIN BY
TONBRIDGE PRINTERS LTD
SHIPBOURNE ROAD, TONBRIDGE
KENT

TO KATE

AUTHOR'S NOTE

The first part of this collection is made up of a few poems from my first book, *Poems* (Fortune Press, 1939): the last part consists of recent and previously uncollected poems. The other parts contain respectively most of the poems in *The Middle of a War* (Hogarth Press, 1942), *A Lost Season* (Hogarth Press, 1944), *Epitaphs and Occasions* (John Lehmann, 1949), *Counterparts* (Derek Verschoyle, 1954) and *Brutus's Orchard* (André Deutsch, 1957). (One or two war-time poems which appeared in *Epitaphs and Occasions* now take their appropriate place).

The poem 'On the Mountain' is greatly indebted to Moses Hadas's translation of Burckhardt's *The Age of Constantine the Great*.

CONTENTS

I

The Journey   *page* 17
Centaurs   18
End of a City   19
To M. S., killed in Spain   20
Ballad of the Last Heir   23
Death   29
The Pure Poet   30
Follower's Song   30
August 1938   31
To My Brother   32

II

Autumn 1939   37
The Barber   37
War Poet   38
Summer 1940   39
To My Wife   41
Autumn 1940   42
Soliloquy in an Air Raid   43
Epitaph on a Bombing Victim   45
ABC of a Naval Trainee   45
The Growth of Crime   46
The Bay   49
Defending the Harbour   49
Autumn 1941   50
Royal Naval Air Station   51
Saturday Night in a Sailors' Home   52
The End of a Leave   52
The Middle of a War   53
Waiting to be Drafted   53
Y.M.C.A. Writing Room   54
Another War   55
Illness of Love   55
Spring 1942   56
Harbour Ferry   56
Good-Bye for a Long Time   57
The Dream   58
Troopship   59

III

In Africa   *page* 63
The Photographs   63
The Green Hills of Africa   64
The Giraffes   65
The Plains   66
Askari's Song   67
The White Conscript and the Black Conscript   68
Natives Working on the Aerodrome   69
The Tribes   69
Teba   70
Autumn 1942   76
Sadness, Theory, Glass   77
What is Terrible   79
A Wry Smile   80
Shore Leave Lorry   81
Upon a Revolutionary Killed in the War   82
Spring 1943   82
War Letters   83
The Coast   84
Night   85
Crustaceans   86
The Petty Officers' Mess   87
Today and Tomorrow   89
The Legions   89
September 3, 1943   90
The Emotion of Fiction   90
The Statue   92
Return   93
Winter in Camp   93
Epitaphs for Soldiers   98
Winter Night   98
During a Bombardment by V-Weapons   99
Epilogue   99

IV

Dedicatory Epistle   103
On Seeing the Leni Riefenstahl Film   107
On Hearing Bartok's Concerto   107
Schwere Gustav   107
Fathers and Sons   108
The Divided Life Re-lived   108

Meditation	*page* 109
Stanzas	110
1948	111
Virtue	112
Epitaph	112
The Lake	112
Knole	114
Chekhov	114
Emily Dickinson	115
Poets	115
Epitaph for a Spy	116
The Hero	116
Image and Fossil	116
The Extending Segment	117
The Five Hamlets	118
Ancestors	118
Little Fable	119
The Family Cat	119
To My Son	120
The Gaze	121
Sleeping and Waking	121
Ballad	122
Nursery Rhyme	122
Song	123
Hymn	124
The Civilization	125
Obituary of R. Fuller	126
Tailpiece	127

V

Rhetoric of a Journey	131
Ten Memorial Poems	134
The Snow	138
Youth Revisited	138
Time	140
Côte des Maures	140
The Image	141
Sentimental Poem	142
Poem to Pay for a Pen	143
The Two Poets	144
To a Notebook	144
Preface to an Anthology	145

On Reading a Soviet Novel   *page* 145
Two Poems from Baudelaire   146
André Gide   147
Ibsen   148
On Spalding's *Handbook to Proust*   149
Necrophagy   149
Translation   150
Inaction   151
Socialist's Song   152
A Wet Sunday in Spring   153
Times of War and Revolution   154
Winter Roundel   154
The Fifties   154
The Meeting   155
Pantomime   156
Death of a Dictator   157
Nino, the Wonder Dog   157
Images of Autumn   158
Poet and Reader   159

VI

Spring Song   163
Summer   164
Pictures of Winter   165
Autobiography of a Lungworm   166
On Grazing a Finger   167
Elementary Philosophy   168
The Day   168
On a Textbook of Surgery   169
To a Girl in the Morning   169
Eclipse   170
Discrepancies   171
Night Piece   172
Ambiguities   174
Expostulation and Inadequate Reply   175
A Song Between Two Shepherds   177
Pleasure Drive   178
Winter World   180
Florestan to Leonora   181
The Ides of March   182
After the Drama   184
Newstead Abbey   185

One and Many   *page* 186
To Shakespeare   187
The Perturbations of Uranus   188
Amateur Film-making   190
Poem out of Character   191
Sitting for a Portrait   192
At a Warwickshire Mansion   193
Dialogue of the Poet and his Talent   195
The Final Period   196
Jag and Hangover   198
To Posterity?   199
To a Friend Leaving for Greece   200
Mythological Sonnets   201

VII

Monologue in Autumn   213
On the Mountain   215
Faustian Sketches   218
The Hittites   231
Versions of Love   231
Three Birds   232
Anatomy of the Poet   234
Meredithian Sonnets   238

I

THE JOURNEY

Torrid blossoms of snow lay on the trees,
　　Rooks courted in the hollow,
The light came like a mirror's flash
　　From even ploughed and fallow.

He'd travelled all day to reach that place,
　　The house of local stone
Below the line of conifers
　　That shadowed it like a spine.

As he reached the gate the sun went down,
　　The frost came with a crackle
And bound the snow on the trees' windward side
　　And the path as hard as metal.

On the gate-posts he saw a carven shield,
　　On each gate the same symbol,
A shield with a carven deathshead in stone.
　　His feet began to stumble.

'I am like a man in an ancient ballad
　　Drawn to the strangest doom.
Oh what will happen to me that thought
　　To live gently from the womb?'

A tree grew in the chimney there
　　Like a flower in a madman's hat,
And the door for a handle grew a hand
　　And an open mouth for a latch.

'Come in, come in, you honest stranger.'
　　'I fear you and I fear—'
'Come in and dry your sodden shoes
　　Before our faggot fire.'

He's passed the door and in the long hall
　　And no fire can he see.
He's up the stairs and in the bedchamber
　　And no need of fire has he.

(17)

For he's wrestling with the hardest sinews of all,
    With strength the most insane,
And he's tangled himself in the long curtains
    That bear the deathshead sign.

In his cracking brain, his tortured thews,
    A little world is burning:
The snow, the treading rooks, the plan
    Of a last mistaken journey.

CENTAURS

The folded land a horse could stamp through
Raised the centaur with lighter hoof.
The glossy vandyke wake of plough

And painted crops were saved: the truth
Is that the centaur did not eat.
The country never set a roof

Amongst its smoky trees; the sweet
Stables of the centaur lay
Quite open to their augean fate.

What of the land's economy,
Its plans to keep alive the beast,
Whose muscular beauty, white and ghostly,

Stood still against the darker boast?
Being half man it would not draw
The plough or bear the summer harvest:

The other half refused the straw
Shelter, and the elements
Commenced to operate the law.

Clouds covered like a scab the blenched,
Raw sky, and from its arching hangar
Slipped bolts that tore the earth to fragments,

Splashing amongst the seething danger
Below the cardboard base the centaur
Had pawed with merely human anger.

END OF A CITY

Birds in the pattern of a constellation,
Blank pale blue sky, white walls of a citadel,
Silence of country without inhabitants.
The shining aqueducts, elaborate drains,
Puffed fountains, cleanse a sheeted culture
Where the greatest movement is the soft
Wear of stone by water that leaves no trace
Of green, coming from static glaciers.

By night in the city, stars like heraldic birds,
The square, the plinth with the sacred articles,
The statue of the shade of Spartacus,
No change appears, the cooling is unheard
Of monuments of easy living in
The dark air. But the crack is widening
Between the sun and moon, the rest and flow,
The vomatorium and immense sewers.

See how the separate layers come to life.
The sloping theatre rolls down its bodies
To mingle with the last act's tragedy
Upon the stage; from tarnished bed both king
And mistress tumble; pens fall from the hands
Of nerveless bureaucrats; and, rubbing sockets
Of eyeless skulls, the naked slaves awake,
Who face another epoch of draining work.

Within the temple sits the noble JA,
Bearded with seaweed and his elephant's legs
Crossed in the droppings. The lamp has long gone out,
The offerings are mouldy and the priests

Dust in the chancel. This was he who ordered
For his tremendous dropsy the sanitation,
But whose emissaries sent timely hence
Brought no green leaf to soothe his helplessness.

This day is surely lucky for the city.
The last trumpet blown with leaking cheeks
Rouses the oldest tenants from their sleep.
They are the ancestors whose tombs were levelled
At the last cataclysm, but they come
Like grass between the stones, but grass like hair,
And growing goatishly along the sewers,
Over the stage, the temple and on JA.

TO M. S., KILLED IN SPAIN

Great cities where disaster fell
In one small night on every house and man,
Knew how to tell the fable from the flesh:
One crying O, his mouth a marble fountain;
Her thigh bones in immortal larva
At compass points, the west and east of love.

Necks bent to look for the seditious geese,
Or over blocks, gazing into freedom;
Heads all alike, short noses, brows
Folded above, the skin a leather brown;
Wrists thick, the finger pads worn down
Building oppression's towering stone.

Now uncovered is the hero,
A tablet marks him where his life leaked out
Through grimy wounds and vapoured into air.
A rusty socket shows where in the night
He crammed his torch and kept by flame at bay
Dark, prowling wolves of thought that frightened him.

The poor outlasted rope and crucifix,
We break the bones that blenched through mastic gold;
And excavate our story, give a twist
To former endings in deliberate metre,
Whose subtle beat our fathers could not count,
Having their agile thumbs too far from fingers.

    I fear the plucking hand
    That from our equal season
    Sent you to war with wrong
    But left me suavely wound
    In the cocoon of reason
    That preluded your wings.

    As the more supple fin
    Found use in crawling, so
    Some new and rapid nerve
    Brought close your flesh to brain,
    Transformed utopia
    To death for human love.

    And my existence must
    Finish through your trauma
    The speechless brute divorce
    Of heart from sculptured bust:
    Turn after five acts' drama
    A placid crumpled face.

I see my friend rising from the tomb,
His simple head swathed in a turban of white cloth.
The vault is spotted with a brownish moss,
One corner broken, fallen to the floor,
Whereon I read SPAIN as he advances like
An invalid, changed terribly with pain.

A quiet room holds him, half raised from the bed,
Eyes big and bright, a waxwork, and the blood
Of waxworks running down his cheek. Two candles
Rock their light. The bed is moving, tilting,
And slips him rigidly to take a new position,
The elbow sharp, the skin a yellow leaf.

The third time he stands against a summer country,
The chestnuts almost black in thunderous air,
The silver green of willows lining dykes
Choked with flesh. He moves along the furrows
With labourer's fingers, spreading death against
The imperishable elements of earth.

What is the meaning of these images?
The wish to leave all natural objects richer,
To quicken the chemistry of earth, to be
Immortal in our children. Such desires
Are bodies in a pit, the rotting and bloody
Backwash of a tidal pestilence.

       The scalpel in my back
       That broke my uneasy dream
       Has extended in a scythe,
       Is passing through the quick,
       Forcing like strychnine
       My body to its curve.

       The future is not waking,
       Nor the name and number
       Of distorted figures, and knowledge
       Of pain. It is the breaking
       Before we slumber
       Of the shaping image.

       So from the nightmare, from
       The death, the war of ghosts,
       Those chosen to go unharmed
       May join the tall city, the swan
       Of changing thoughts
       Set sailing by the doomed.

BALLAD OF THE LAST HEIR

Lord Ashby the eldest son came down
  And sprawled beside the shallow lake;
He saw the acres of his reversion
  In planes about, immaculate.

No blade had wrinkled the green parkland
  And grazing only were the hunters
With yellow bilious eyeballs, threshing
  Tails, a black company of haunters.

'These lands are bound to my ancient father
  And I am the next to inherit them.
The hunt will ride over his deathbed –
  And over my own in a little time.

'To the vault in the nave of that grey church
  With the names carved there that are my own,
To the yew trees out of tenant and serf
  In the graveyard growing heavy and green
I am bound like a falling stone to earth.

'My face has a history but no future,
  The dead compiled the chivalrous usage,
Raping for ever love and ambition,
  And only time rots their marble visage.

'The heirlooms are clasped by a savage law
  On the body of any that I may love;
The sombre settings and florid gems
  Will spoil young flesh with stain and groove.

'No wanton girl like a slender fish
  Will slip from my bed with a harlot's mime:
I am empty of lust, a grotesque form
  Evolved by a clumsy inbred line.'

Ashby rose up and saw the sun
  Between the trees and the grey church tower
Like a gout of blood on an egg-blue skin,
  An image of internecine war.

He left the lake on his sinister hand,
  Treading a path between the yews:
A bird flew swiftly under the branches
  And down the dark glade beyond his view.

He pressed on the wormy door and drew
  The dusty scarlet cloth aside
And entered the spacious gloom of the church
  With a gleam on brass and flowers relieved.

The sanitary neatness of Bedlam was there,
  A dry spare skull with the brains all gone:
The arches frugally preserved
  Against a greater, a final ruin.

Ashby confronted the fatuous altar,
  The plain high windows of dove-grey light:
The strength of his empty face was the eyes
  Like those a sculptor dared not sight.

But quickly against the reredos,
  Flooding its ghostly alabaster,
A magnesium bud of flaming fiercely
  Showed his pupils who was master.

A cord of terror combed his scalp.
  The symbol snaked and burned dull red
And faded in the theatrical glare
Of pouring light, where dust and where
  The explosion's smoke crepitated and coiled.

Then in the glow stood a solid figure
  With clothes stained red as though in wine,

And from the forehead, like pallid fungus,
Two horns grew in the shape of fingers.
  The ported appendage was silky and fine.

'I know you, Ashby, I know your sorrow.'
  Ashby had gone had he but dared.
The lips of the apparition smiled
  And shaped like butter the separate words.

'Throw off your fear and tradition, Ashby.
  A man should often welcome the devil.'
'Frankly I fear you,' Lord Ashby replied,
  'And tradition tells me you are evil.'

'Your tradition is dead, I'll give you a better.
  The gold of your settings will run in its flame,
The dross be purged from your mouldering gems
  And the land reveal a more fertile loam.

'Your riches are static, I'll make them flow.'
  'What good will avail, my heart's the hurt?'
'It lies in stiff unyielding cerements
  And must be freed if it must beat.'

'But what would you want of me in exchange?'
  'And what would you give me?' the devil said.
'I'll give you a share of the new-minted wealth.'
  'Then sign the bond in your own fine blood.'

'You'll control the way my bread is got.'
  'Cake,' said the devil, his eyes aslant.
'And that you'll determine my way of life
  Is patent from your own argument.'

'O specious youth to apply the standards
  Of hoary winter to your new spring.
Under my rule my laws are good;
  The argument shows that morals are shifting.'

(25)

The trees brushed against the arching windows,
   A thin wind jangled a ghost of bells.
The devil gathered his hired red robes.
'This place is haunted'. He twitched the lobes
   Of his pointed ears. 'Grasp my shoulders well.

'I'll show you the forge for your raw rich lumber,
   The boundless realm of our company;
Strange food to stop your foolish mouth
   And passion to fill your questioning eye.'

Then Ashby hung on the devil's shoulders:
   He smelt the heat of the body's rages,
The dust from the woollen scarlet cloak,
   An odour of shoddy provincial stages.

Then he saw the altar far beneath
   And soon the grey church tower, the trees,
The toy horses and the pleasure grounds,
   Until the half light smeared these views.

The devil turned his animal head
   And spoke with the cold diluted air.
'The winking limits of aerodrome
The dark north prick like a waking dream
   With wings you will inherit there.

'And to the south the esplanade
   Of the sweet immoral watering place,
A glittering snake coiled round the bight,
Promises a press of thighs in moonlight,
   A bright moist path to Dian's grace.'

They flew until Lord Ashby could see
   The yellow slots of factory windows,
And they rested upon a grey slag heap
   To see the town's industrial wonders.

The gas lit streets were laid with cobbles,
    Their people a pale diminutive race.
'These are the craftsmen of your metal.'
    'I fear the bitter collective face.'

'They are the genii of the ring,
    They are phantoms with only strength to slave.'
'I have no confidence in oppression
    And strength is a menace without their love.

'If our kingdom should rest on these Nibelungs
    I think our reign is brief indeed.'
'You will not again view this crude country,
    Its vapours require a healthier breed.

'I'll save your aristocratic frame
    From the shocks of such elemental scenes.
Your function is not to produce but dispose:
    You should not be hampered by questions of means.'

Then Ashby's uneasy flesh was borne
    Across one squalid eaten face
Of the serf-made pyramid of power.
    He turned his eyes from the smoky place.

The glow of the forge fell back in the dark,
    The high-pitched rattle of spindles ceased,
The slow death in the oppressive house
    Tinctured the final narrow street.

In the velvet of the upper air,
    Curving a planetary path,
The devil, his arm supporting Ashby,
    Attempted to sooth the startled youth.

'Your home is a palace of many rooms,
    Its porcelain walls trap cool white air,
In shapely pots are luxuriant posies,
Tongued orchids and soft ceruminous roses,
    And waxen ivy wreaths the stair.

(27)

'You mount to the roof with an airman's eye
  Of the sunlit landscape, flat as paving,
And in the middle distance find
The necessary objects waving
  Tendrils of parasites under sand.

'The sphinx as lover with flawless breasts,
  The broken lintels of exchanges,
A novel machine in idleness,
Arranged in isolation replace
  Rough nature's wasteful wearing hinges.

'Breaking the quivering horizon stands,
  In lovely visual form, the trust
Of death, a marble skyscraper,
  Lonely devourer of the rest.'

The devil produced from his narrow bosom
  A parchment and a pointed reed.
'You sign and touch this seal and say
  "I deliver this my act and deed".'

The devil's gesture had swift effect.
  'You've taken me from my own country,
From the dusty cherry and phallic chestnut
  That in spring would have delighted me.

'You've saved me from the dreaded symbols:
  The flattened rabbit in the road,
The yellow winds in the cutting fall,
  Blunt proper knives for scraping scab.

'You promised me freedom where I had none.
  Let me return to the entailed land.'
Lord Ashby's words were hurried and shrill.
'For I will not live in your insane hell.'
  Some white showed on the other's hand.

They were falling with the falling sky
   And the globe's gear began to engage with them.
The devil said 'You damned aristo,
   Mine was a decent charity home.

'The last of your race in a tottering house,
   The door grown over with lurid weeds,
Whom do you think would succeed to the corpse,
   The broken stones and moss-blanked words?

'If you want the truth, you are useless, a ghost.'
   'And what are you but a superstition?'
'Die!' screamed the devil. 'I'll steal your world.'
   'Then inherit,' said Ashby, 'a realm of attrition.'

The devil loosed his supporting arm
   And the boy whirled down from the dark domain
Like a parachute after the turning earth,
A fluttering convulsive effort at birth:
   But below were scattered his bright remains.

DEATH

How many doors will this man open
And stand with his skull against the light
And move his reddened eyes like hyphens
On the tight parchment of his face,

Insert his stick and grasp the post
And lift his legs over the threshold
And let his free hand, white as chalk,
As cold as sculpture, hang like cheese?

The number of his entrances
Is known: the door will shortly open
And he will not be there, the light
Will shine into the room and back

Along the straight corridor upon
Himself advancing with some hope
Towards the gateposts and the void
(Between them) of his older shape.

THE PURE POET

He spoke of poetry: his lips had shrunk
To lines across the gums: he also stank.
He said that since the Greeks few had the gifts,
That syphilis and lice were perquisites.
He brought a charnel breath and spotted cloths,
The swansdown shroud was fluttered when he coughed
His postulate of the sufficient word.
I felt viridian when he launched on blood,
Perceived the surgery behind the trance,
That his long travels in pursuit of tense
Were clearly all compelled by social syntax;
And but for his unpleasant human antics
I could have pitied him for being dead.
Still he sat on and told me how he made
His money, villa, servants, the model globe,
His regular habits and the seven-faced cube.
Further I could not follow him, among
The obscure allusions to important dung,
Nor as at length he tried a final scare
And vanished through the non-existent door.

FOLLOWER'S SONG

Oh to be simple and give the salute,
To be hopeful and happy,
For life to be sucked through the root
And the branches sappy.

Oh to be mad with marching and May,
To be bold, to be brutish,
To dream in the night and by day
To delight in duties.

And oh for the pointing finger to cube
To a gun and the feeling
Inside to come out of the tube
And kill with its healing;

The earth to be gone with its grave and the sky
With its season: forever
To shake in God's voice and to lie
Next his iron and leather.

AUGUST 1938

Mapping this bay and charting
The water's ribby base
By individual smarting
And walks in shifting sand,
We note the official place;
Dover with pursed up lips
Behind the purple land
Blowing her little ships
To danger, large and bland:

Aeroplanes softly landing
Beyond the willowed marsh:
The sexy lighthouse standing
Aloof with rolling eye
From shingle flat and harsh:
And sequinned on the coast
Beneath the usual sky
The pleasure towns where most
Have come to live or die.

Far off the quinsied Brenner,
The open hungry jaw
Of Breslau and Vienna
Through day-old papers join
The mood of tooth and claw
To useless coastal road,

The excursion to Boulogne
And valedictory ode,
The hairy untanned groin.

Oh never is forever
Over this curving ground
When both the dull and clever
Leave for their town of graves,
And on the dissolving mound
By snowy seabirds signed
'Through all routes quit these waves,'
Lonely among his kind
The local spirit raves.

TO MY BROTHER

A pistol is cocked and levelled in the room.
The running window opens to the sounds
Of hooters from the Thames at Greenwich, doom

Descends the chimney in the rustling grounds
Of soot. The Globe edition of Pope you gave me
Is open on the chair arm. There are bounds

To feeling in this suburb, but nothing can save me
Tonight from the scenic railway journey over
Europe to locate my future grave: the

Arming world rushes by me where you hover
Behind right shoulders on the German border,
Or at the *Terminus* removing a cover,

Taking perhaps your memories, like a warder,
The memories of our responsible youth,
To give the refugees a sense of order.

My real world also has a base of truth:
Soldiers with labial sores, a yellowish stone
Built round the common into cubes, uncouth

Reverberations from a breaking bone,
The fear of living in the body. Is it
Here we start or end? Tonight my own

Thoughts pay a merely temporary visit
To the state where objects have lost their power of motion,
Their laws which terrify and can elicit

A furious tale from casual emotion,
Where life with instruments surveys the maps
Of cutout continent and plasticine ocean,

Far from the imminent and loud collapse
Of culture, prophesied by liberals,
Whose guilty ghosts can never say perhaps.

This kind of world Pope, with his quartz and shells,
Constructed in his azure Twickenham grotto,
Which in the day time entertained the belles,

But glowed and writhed to form a personal motto
At night, with brute distraction in its lair;
The mirrors flattering as part of the plot: 'O

Alex, you are handsome; you have power
First to arrange a world and then to abstract
Its final communication; virtues shower

From the exercise of your genius; the pact
Of friendship is good and all your enemies only
In opposition to civilisation act.'

When I am falsely elevated and lonely,
And the effort of making contact even with you
Is helped by distance, the life is finely

Shown which holds on contract, and the true
Perish in cities which revolve behind
Like dust.
              The window explodes, and now
The centre land mass breathes a tragic wind.

II

II

AUTUMN 1939

Cigar-coloured bracken, the gloom between the trees,
The straight wet by-pass through the shaven clover,
Smell of the war as if already these
   Were salient or cover.

The movements of people are directed by
The officious finger of the gun and their
Desires are sent like squadrons in the sky,
   Uniform and bare.

I see a boy through the reversing lens
Wearing a shirt the colour of his gums;
His face lolls on the iron garden fence
   Slobbering his thumbs.

I have no doubt that night is real which creeps
Over the concrete, that murder is fantasy,
That what should now inform the idiot sleeps
   Frozen and unfree.

THE BARBER

Reading the shorthand on a barber's sheet
In a warm and chromium basement in Cannon Street
I discovered again the message of the city,
That without power there is no place for pity.

The barber with a flat and scented hand
Moved the dummy's head in its collar band.
'What will you do with the discarded hair?'

The mirror showed a John the Baptist's face,
Detached and sideways. 'Can you tell me how,'
It said, 'I may recover grace?

'Make me a merchant, make me a manager.'
His scissors mournfully declined the task.
'Will you do nothing that I ask?'

'It is no use,' he said, 'I cannot speak
To you as one in a similar position.
For me you are the stern employer,
Of wealth the accumulator.
I must ignore your singular disposition.'

He brushed my shoulders and under his practised touch
I knew his words were only a deceit.
'You spoke to me according to the rules
Laid down for dealing with madmen and with fools.'

'I do my best,' he said, 'my best is sufficient.
If I have offended it is because
I never formulate the ideal action
Which depends on observation.'

'And do you never observe and never feel
Regret at the destruction of wealth by war?
Do you never sharpen your razor on your heel
And draw it across selected throats?'

He smiled and turned away to the row of coats.
'This is your mackintosh,' he said, 'you had no hat.
Turn left for the station and remember the barber.
There is just time enough for that.'

WAR POET

Swift had pains in his head.
Johnson dying in bed
Tapped the dropsy himself.
Blake saw a flea and an elf.
Tennyson could hear the shriek
Of a bat. Pope was a freak.
Emily Dickinson stayed
Indoors for a decade.
Water inflated the belly
Of Hart Crane, and of Shelley.
Coleridge was a dope.

Southwell died on a rope.
Byron had a round white foot.
Smart and Cowper were put
Away. Lawrence was a fidget.
Keats was almost a midget.
Donne, alive in his shroud,
Shakespeare, in the coil of a cloud,
Saw death very well as he
Came crab-wise, dark and massy.
I envy not only their talents
And fertile lack of balance
But the appearance of choice
In their sad and fatal voice.

SUMMER 1940

I

Charing Cross: where trains depart for the bombardment
And the leave-taking is particularly ardent;
The obelisk in the court-yard is streaming with lime,
The doves are crying in the dusk, and Time

Says: *I am money, I am all these people,*
The quality in light which changes to purple
When goods have been left with the owner of the mill
And the authority is his to sell.

I wipe my fingers on the hurrying faces,
And implant the wish to be in different places.
I am Too Late, I am the trees which grow
In everyone and blossom pale and grey.

II

The edges of the country are fraying with
Too much use; the ports are visited by wrath
In the shapes of the metal diver and the dart
With screaming feathers and explosive heart.

And the ships are guilty of a desire to return
To land, to three mile pits and the moulding urn.
England no longer is shaped like a begging dog,
Its shape is the shape of a state in the central bog,

With frontiers which change at the yawn of a tired ruler;
At last the push of time has reached it; realer
Today than for centuries, England is on the map
As a place where something occurs, as a spring-board or trap.

Oh what is to happen? Does that depend on Time
Alone? Will change of country eventually come
As slow erosion by the wind of mountains,
And of love as the green-slimed Cupid of the fountain?

Only people and not places are able to resist
Time for a space, to race their daily ghost
In the projectile of violent change: the power
Is in the people to pool their collective hours,

And reply to Time: *You are not all the people,*
You are the weak man underneath the steeple,
You are the exploiter and appropriator,
The hurt philosopher who murmurs Later,

You are all those who assisted death, who weighted
The curve with war and a system of hatred.
You are condemned as a reward or lash,
As an explosion, as a fear or wish.

III

Will you depart now? Will you become a place?
There is really no penalty, there may be peace.
Will you add yourself in the calculation of
The perimeter, the coast-line lost to love?

The third voice says this; it is almost our own.
The voice of pigeons as they drop from stone,
From the cornices of banks, the premises
Of rings and trusts, from all betrayed promises;

The voice of wings attractive to the cripple,
The soothing voice of tobacco-pipe and nipple,
Of introvert ambition which Icarus heard,
The voice of the weeping and isolated bird.

TO MY WIFE

The loud mechanical voices of the sirens
Lure me from sleep and on the heath, like stars,
Moths fall into a mounting shaft of light.
Aircraft whirr over and then the night stays quiet;
The moon is peeled of cloud, its gold is changed
On stone for silver and the cap of sky
Glitters like quartz, impersonal and remote.
This surface is the same: the clock's bland face,
Its smiling moustaches, hide the spring, knotted
Like muscles, and the crouching jungle hammer.

The same but so different with you not here.
This evening when I turned from the clothes you left,
Empty and silk, the souls of swallows flickered
Against the glass of our house: I felt no better
Along the tree-massed alleys where I saw
The long pale legs on benches in the dark.
It was no vague nostalgia which I breathed
Between the purple colloids of the air:
My lust was as precise and fierce as that of
The wedge-headed jaguar or the travelling Flaubert.

But I only encountered the ghosts of the suburb,
Those ghosts you know and who are real and walk
And talk in the small public gardens, by the tawdry
Local monuments; the Witch and Big Head
And the others, fleeting and familiar as
Our memories and ambitions, and just as dead.
Being alone they stopped me; Big Head first.
Removing her unbelievable hat, she showed me
What before I had only conjectured, and she whispered:
O lucky you – you might have been born like this.

I knew it was true, but, hurrying on, the Witch
Lifted her cane and barred the way: she is
Lean and very dirty but hanging round
That skeleton are rags of flesh still handsome.
Moving her lips madly and in a foreign tone she said:
Oh do not hope, boy – you will come to this.
I ran, being certain that she had not erred,
Back to our room where now the only noise
Is the icy modulated voice of Mozart
And the false clock ticking on the mantelpiece.

Now in the bubble of London whose glass will soon
Smear into death, at the still-calm hour of four,
I see the shadows of our life, the Fates
We narrowly missed, our possible destiny.
I try to say that love is more solid than
Our bodies, but I only want you here.
*I know they created love and that the rest
Is ghosts; war murders love – I really say.*
But dare I write it to you who have said it
Always and have no consolation from the ghosts?

AUTUMN 1940

No longer can guns be cancelled by love,
Or by rich paintings in the galleries;
The music in the icy air cannot live,
The autumn has blown away the rose.

Can we be sorry that those explosions
Which occurring in Spain and China reached us as
The outer ring of yearning emotions,
Are here as rubble and fear, as metal and glass,

Are here in the streets, in the sewers full of people?
We see as inevitable and with relief
The smoke from shells like plump ghosts on the purple,
The bombers, black insect eggs, on the sky's broad leaf.

For these are outside the deathly self
Walking where leaves are spun across the lips
Bitten against tears which bridge no gulf,
Where swans on the flat full river are moving
                              like oared ships.

Death is solitary and creeps along the Thames
At seven, with mists and changing moons;
Death is in the music and the paintings, the dreams
Still amorous among the dispersing guns.

But where the many are there is no death,
Only a temporary expedient of sorrow
And destruction; today the caught-up breath –
The exhalation is promised for tomorrow.

And changed tomorrow is promised precisely by
The measure of the engendered hate, the hurt
Descended; the instinct and capacity
Of man for happiness, and that drowned art.

SOLILOQUY IN AN AIR RAID

The will dissolves, the heart becomes excited,
Skull suffers formication; moving words
Fortuitously issue from my hand.
The winter heavens, seen all day alone,
Assume the colour of aircraft over the phthisic
Guns.

But who shall I speak to with this poem?

Something was set between the words and the world
I watched today; perhaps the necrotomy
Of love or the spectre of pretence; a vagueness;
But murdering their commerce like a tariff.

Inside the poets the words are changed to desire,
And formulations of feeling are lost in action
Which hourly transmutes the basis of common speech.

(43)

Our dying is effected in the streets,
London an epicentrum; to the stench
And penny prostitution in the shelters
Dare not extend the hospital and bogus
Hands of propaganda.

                              Ordered this year:
A billion tons of broken glass and rubble,
Blockade of chaos, the other requisites
For the reduction of Europe to a rabble.
Who can observe this save as a frightened child
Or careful diarist? And who can speak
And still retain the tones of civilization?
The verse that was the speech of observation –
Jonson's cartoon of the infant bourgeoisie,
Shakespeare's immense assertion that man alone
Is almost the equal of his environment,
The Chinese wall of class round Pope, the Romantic
Denunciation of origin and mould –
Is sunk in the throat between the opposing voices:

I am the old life, which promises even less
In the future, and guarantees your loss.

And I the new, in which your function and
Your form will be dependent on my end.

Kerensky said of Lenin: *I must kindly*
Orientate him to what is going on.
Watching the images of fabulous girls
On cinema screens, the liberal emotion
Of the slightly inhuman poet wells up in me,
As irrelevant as Kerensky. It is goodbye
To the social life which permitted melancholy
And madness in the isolation of its writers,
To a struggle as inconclusive as the Hundred
Years' War. The air, as welcome as morphia,
This 'rich ambiguous aesthetic air'
Which now I breathe, is an effective diet

Only for actors: in the lonely box
The author mumbles to himself, the play
Unfolds spontaneous as the human wish,
As autumn dancing, vermilion on rocks.

EPITAPH ON A BOMBING VICTIM

Reader, could his limbs be found
Here would lie a common man:
History inflicts no wound
But explodes what it began,
And with its enormous lust
For division splits the dust.
Do not ask his nation; that
Was History's confederate.

ABC OF A NAVAL TRAINEE

A is the anger we hide with some danger,
Keeping it down like the twentieth beer.
B is the boredom we feel in this bedlam.
C is the cautious and supervised cheer.

D is the tea dope and E English duping,
Too feeble for folly, too strong for revolt.
F is the adjective near every object,
The chief of desires for both genius and dolt.

G is the gun which can kill at, say, Greenwich
If fired at St Martin's, and H is our hate
Non-existent behind it wherever we wind it.
I is the image of common man's fate.

J is the Joan or the Jill or Joanna,
Appearing in dreams as a just missed train.
K is the kindness like Christmas tree candles,
Unexpected and grateful as poppies in grain.

L is the lung or the limb which in languor
Rests after work and will soon be exposed
To M which is murder, a world rather madder,
Where what we pretend now's as real as your nose.

N is the nightingale's song that we're noting
When the sky is a lucid darkening silk,
When the guns are at rest and the heart is a cancer
And our mouths make O at the moon of milk.

Then we remember, no longer a number,
We think of our duties as poets and men:
Beyond us lie Paris, Quebec, Rome, where diaries
Of millions record the same troubles and pain.

S is the silence for brooding on violence.
T is the toughness imparted to all.
U is the unit that never will clown it
Again as the lonely, the shy or the tall.

V is the vastness: as actor and witness
We double our role and stammer at first.
W is war to start off the quarries –
Our everyday hunger and every night thirst.

X is the kiss or the unknown, the fissure
In misery stretching far back to the ape.
Y is the yearning for Eden returning;
Our ending, our Z and our only escape.

THE GROWTH OF CRIME

A sailor walks along the street,
His cap a halo on his head:
Out of a squalid window gleam
Curved surfaces of skin and red
Paint that profligate women use
And the brass knobs of a bed.

'Sailor, come in,' a soft voice calls.
Behind the house the night comes on
And each cloud on the blenching sky
Darkens and feels for the other one,
And down the road the docks grow dark;
The unmuffled noises of day are gone.

Bounding the town is the acid sea
Which nibbles the plates of the plying ships;
They fall down hills of black-green glass,
Are suspended on summits curled like whips,
And from rigging and gun, like a leaky house,
From body and clothing the grey sea drips.

'Come in, come in.' The voice is plucking
Softly the horizontal air.
The searchlights start to stain the night,
A trembling hum is everywhere.
He imagines the sea a film of blood,
Lopped bodies the shadows on the stair.

And through the walls the whispering
Of lovers, the crying, the old, the bored,
Comes like a touch to his ears. 'The rope
Keeps breaking.' 'I hate to be adored.'
'Give me death but take this pain.'
'Can we afford it? Can we afford?'

He climbs and enters the rose-lit room:
She smiles at him and does not move.
He sits beside her and sees the smile:
He looks at his hand in the shape of a dove,
His breathing trunk, his alien limbs.
And hides in her, crying: 'My love, my love.'

The images of waking brush
Like branches his suddenly staring eyes.
The room is dark, the processions go
Of distorted passion, haunting lies,
From window to bed, and make the world
Fearful as origin and as size.

And sleeping still beside him is
The woman: in her sleeping mask
The worm of his confessions grows.
What has he told her? What did he ask?
This sordid boneless oyster flesh
Is one of his symbols; the cave, the flask.

Some secret lives behind the brambles,
The wine brims up and can be spilled.
Madness and hatred grow in a night:
Strumpets are lonely and can be killed:
Nothing reminds him of day and its reason,
The logic of night, the violence that's willed.

Instead the voices in each ear
Are saying what he has never dared:
'Within its herded operatives
War swells and petrifies the bared
Egotistical and violent soul:
Fear and horror cannot be shared.

Each one has only his little world
Of sensuousness and memory,
And endeavours with the ghastly shell,
The savage skin, the cruel eye,
To save it: in that animal's
Rank den and bed of love it dies.'

He stops his ears; he moves the blind:
The common objects of the room
Glow like the rows of watching faces
In a theatre's powdered violet gloom;
The woman's shape beneath the sheets
Is a gross and convoluted bloom.

The empty bottles point their fingers,
The idiot clothes lie on the floor:
The time is the endless hinge of night,
The opening, slow and living door:
He puts his face near hers as though
To see the grinning yellow core.

She mutters: 'Here in my breast; I have had it
Ever' and 'Oh, horrible!' she cries.
Then from her sleep she moves into
The inch between, as wide as skies.
And he upon their opening sees
Death half an hour behind her eyes.

THE BAY

The semi-circular and lunar bay
Where tumbling, grey stones meet untidily
The grey volcanic waves: no man, no tree,
Breaks the cold greenness of the bitten lea –
This scene the orator of memory
Already knew: forbore till now to say.

But on the hill the gun's black twig, the moan
Of the convoy home from seas instinct with steel,
The hidden spies, the bomber's slanting keel
As slowly it takes the wind – all these remain
Unwished, undreamed, unknown. They are the days,
The escaping seconds, terrible and real,
Through which I live; which memory will seal
To keep and smear for ever future bays.

DEFENDING THE HARBOUR

We form a company to help defend
The harbour. Close against the quay a landed
Monster of a trawler huddles, grey, with sides
Flaking, and aft a grey untidy gun.
Mist shines the cobbles, dulls our waiting boots.

A climbing street links sea and town: we watch
Its pathetic burden of human purpose. All
The faces in my section are thumbed and known
As a pack of cards, and all the characters
Group and speak like a bad familiar play.

And nothing happens but the passage of time,
The monotonous wave on which we are borne and hope
Will never break. But we suspect already
The constant ache as something malignant and
Descry unspeakable deeps in the boring sand.

And on the quay, in our imagination,
The grass of starvation sprouts between the stones,
And ruins are implicit in every structure.
Gently we probe the kind and comic faces
For the strength of heroes and for martyrs' bones.

AUTUMN 1941

The objects are disposed: the sky is suitable.
Where the coast curves the waves' blown smoke
Blurs with the city's and the pencilled ships
Lumber like toys. The searchers for coal and driftwood
Bend; and the beach is littered with stones and leaves,
Antlers of seaweed, round gulls, to the belt
Of sand, like macadam, watered by the sea.

Well then? It is here one asks the question.
Here, under such a sky, with just that menace of purple,
One confronts the varieties of death and of people
With a certain sense of their inadequacy;
And the grandeur of historical conceptions,
The wheeling empires, appearance of lusty classes,
The alimentary organizations, the clever
Extrications from doom, seize the imagination
As though these forms, as gods, existed cruel,
Aloof, but eventually for our salvation.
And, like the shapes themselves of nature or
The inexorable patterns of nightmare, days
And the sequence of days pull our untidy acts
Into the formidable expression of time and destiny.
The tumbling ocean humps itself to Europe –
There the machines, the armies and the skies,

The stains of movement and the burning regions,
Have all the echoes of a myth and in
My blood reside inhuman power and guilt,
Whose fathers made both myth and progeny.

How will this end? The answer is not in doubt;
For the mood at last plunges to earth like a shot airman:
The only truth is the truth of graves and mirrors.
And people walk about with death inside them
Beseeching the poets to make it real. The sea,
The desolate sea, divides; the heavens are
Perpetual; and the city with its million
Falls to its knees in the sand. O heroes, comrades,
The world is no vision and is devoid of ghosts.

ROYAL NAVAL AIR STATION

The piano, hollow and sentimental, plays,
And outside, falling in a moonlit haze,
The rain is endless as the empty days.

Here in the mess, on beds, on benches, fall
The blue serge limbs in shapes fantastical:
The photographs of girls are on the wall.

And the songs of the minute walk into our ears;
Behind the easy words are difficult tears:
The pain which stabs is dragged out over years.

A ghost has made uneasy every bed.
You are not you without me and *The dead
Only are pleased to be alone* it said.

And hearing it silently the living cry
To be again themselves, or sleeping try
To dream it is impossible to die.

SATURDAY NIGHT IN A SAILORS' HOME

A honeycomb of cabins, boxes, cells,
To which each man retires alone.
A snatch of singing, like a groan,
Broken off quickly. Sour, damp smells.

The cell is never dark. There are
The drummings of fluid on enamel.
Behind the separating panel
The anxious voices speak in prayer:

I wish I could be sick and *Please
Shake me at five: God, what an hour
To wake!* The drugs have lost their power:
Still crawling in the naked light
Are the obscene realities.
The coughing goes on all the night.

THE END OF A LEAVE

Out of the damp black light,
The noise of locomotives,
A thousand whispering –
Sharp-nailed, sinewed, slight,
I meet that alien thing
Your hand, with all its motives.

Far from the roof of night
And iron these encounter;
In the gigantic hall
As the severing light
Menaces – human, small,
These hands exchange their counters.

Suddenly our relation
Is terrifyingly simple
Against our wretched times,
Like a hand which mimes
Love in this anguished station
Against a whole world's pull.

THE MIDDLE OF A WAR

My photograph already looks historic.
The promising youthful face, the matelot's collar,
Say 'This one is remembered for a lyric.
His place and period – nothing could be duller.'

Its position is already indicated –
The son or brother in the album; pained
The expression and the garments dated,
His fate so obviously preordained.

The original turns away: as horrible thoughts,
Loud fluttering aircraft slope above his head
At dusk. The ridiculous empires break like biscuits.
Ah, life has been abandoned by the boats –
Only the trodden island and the dead
Remain, and the once inestimable caskets.

WAITING TO BE DRAFTED

It might be any evening of spring;
The air is level, twilight in a moment
Will walk behind us and his shadow
    Fall cold across our day.

The usual trees surround an empty field
And evergreens and gravel frame the house;
Primroses lie like tickets on the ground;
    The mauve island floats on grey.

My senses are too sharp for what the mind
Presents them. In this common scene reside
Small elements with power to agitate
    And move me like a play.

I have watched a young stray dog with an affection
Of the eyes, and seen it peer from the encrusted
Lids, like a man, before it ran towards me,
    Unreasonably gay.

And watched it gnawing at a scrap of leather
In its hunger, and afterwards lying down,
Its ineffectual paws against its cracks
    Of eyes, as though to pray.

Pity and love one instant and the next
Disgust, and constantly the sense of time
Retreating, leaving events like traps: I feel
    This always, most today.

My comrades are in the house, their bodies are
At the mercy of time, their minds are nothing but
                              yearning.
From windows where they lie, as from quiet water,
    The light is taken away.

Y.M.C.A. WRITING ROOM

A map of the world is on the wall: its lying
Order and compression shadow these bent heads.
Here we try to preserve communications;
The maps mocks us with dangerous blues and reds.

Today my friends were drafted; they are about
To be exploded, to be scattered over
That coloured square which in reality
Is a series of scenes, is boredom, cover,

Nostalgia, labour, death. They will explore
Minutely particular deserts, seas and reefs,
Invest a thousand backcloths with their moods,
And all will carry, like a cancer, grief.

In England at this moment the skies contain
Ellipses of birds within their infinite planes,
At night the ragged patterns of the stars;
And distant trees are like the branching veins

Of an anatomical chart: as menacing
As pistols the levelled twigs present their buds.
They have exchanged for this illusion of danger
The ordeal of walking in the sacred wood.

The season cannot warm them nor art console.
These words are false as the returning Spring
From which this March history has made subtraction:
The spirit has gone and left the marble thing.

ANOTHER WAR

Pity, repulsion, love and anger,
The vivid allegorical
Reality of gun and hangar,
Sense of the planet's imminent fall:

Our fathers felt these things before
In another half-forgotten war.

And our emotions are caught part
From them; their weaponed world it is
They should have left to the abyss
Or made an image of their heart.

ILLNESS OF LOVE

Love, the invaders of your mortal shape,
The thought of those marauders, chill me so
That now, as you lie helpless and asleep,
Only my fear is real and ghostly go
The bed, the chair, the clothes and all the rest
Of this particular moment of our story –
The slender guns, the nervous purple coast,
The time of war which is the time of history.

When I imagine I could lose to death
Those scraps of life I shored against my weakness,
The balancing of self upon events
Becomes irrelevant art, a waste of breath;
That weakness nothing when through fearful darkness,
Apish, its frame as though through jungle pants.

SPRING 1942

Once as we were sitting by
The falling sun, the thickening air,
The chaplain came against the sky
And quietly took a vacant chair.

And under the tobacco smoke:
'Freedom,' he said, and 'Good' and 'Duty.'
We stared as though a savage spoke.
The scene took on a singular beauty.

And we made no reply to that
Obscure, remote communication,
But only looked out where the flat
Meadow dissolved in vegetation.

And thought: O sick, insatiable
And constant lust; O death, our future;
O revolution in the whole
Of human use of man and nature!

HARBOUR FERRY

The oldest and simplest thoughts
Rise with the antique moon:
How she enamels men
And artillery under her sphere,
Eyelids and hair and throats
Rigid in love and war;
How this has happened before.

And how the lonely man
Raises his head and shudders
With a brilliant sense of the madness,
The age and shape of his planet,
Wherever his human hand,
Whatever his set of tenets,
The long and crucial minute.

Tonight the moon has risen
Over a quiet harbour,
Through twisted iron and labour,
Lighting the half-drowned ships.
Oh surely the fatal chasm
Is closer, the furious steps
Swifter? The silver drips

From the angle of the wake:
The moon is flooding the faces.
The moment is over: the forces
Controlling lion nature
Look out of the eyes and speak:
*Can you believe in a future
Left only to rock and creature?*

GOOD-BYE FOR A LONG TIME

A furnished room beyond the stinging of
The sea, reached by a gravel road in which
Puddles of rain stare up with clouded eyes:

The photographs of other lives than ours;
The scattered evidence of your so brief
Possession; daffodils fading in a vase.

Our kisses here as they have always been,
Half sensual, half sacred, bringing like
A scent our years together, crowds of ghosts.

And then among the thousand thoughts of parting
The kisses grow perfunctory; the years
Are waved away by your retreating arm.

And now I am alone. I am once more
The far-off boy without a memory,
Wandering with an empty deadened self.

Suddenly under my feet there is the small
Body of a bird, startling against the gravel.
I see its tight shut eye, a trace of moisture,

And, ruffling its gentle breast the wind, its beak
Sharpened by death: and I am yours again,
Hurt beyond hurting, never to forget.

THE DREAM

I dreamed of my child's face, all bloody.
Waking, I heard
The tortured creak of wood, the whistling
Like some night-haunting, death-presaging bird.

O terrifying life that might
Do hurt to him
And sets me helpless on this ship,
Hub of the whirling ocean's constant rim.

And worse: allows the happy past
To hide in that distorting mind
Where sleep alone
Can make it realer than the world-blown wind.

TROOPSHIP

Now the fish fly, the multiple skies display
Still more astounding patterns, the colours are
More brilliant than fluid paint, the grey more grey.

At dawn I saw a solitary star
Making a wake across the broken sea,
Against the heavens swayed a sable spar.

The hissing of the deep is silence, the
Only noise is our memories.

                     O far
From our desires, at every torrid port,
Between the gem-hung velvet of the waves,
Our sires and grandsires in their green flesh start,
Bend skinny elbows, warn: 'We have no graves.
We passed this way, with good defended ill.
Our virtue perished, evil is prince there still.'

III

III

IN AFRICA

Parabolas of grief, the hills are never
Hills and the plains,
Where through the torrid air the lions shiver,
No longer plains.

Just as the lives of lions now are made
Shabby with rifles,
This great geography shrinks into sad
And personal trifles.

For those who are in love and are exiled
Can never discover
How to be happy: looking upon the wild
They see for ever

The cultivated acre of their pain;
The clouds like dreams,
Involved, improbable; the endless plain
Precisely as it seems.

THE PHOTOGRAPHS

The faces in the obscene photographs
Gaze out with no expression: they are like
The dead, who always look as though surprised
In a most intimate attitude. The man
And woman in the photograph have faces
Of corpses; their positions are of love –
Which we have taken. I remember how
Once, coming from the waves, I found you chill
Beneath the *maillot* in a sun-warmed house;
And on such memories are now imposed
The phantasies engendered by these two.

Evening: the rows of anxious aircraft wait,
Speckled with tiny brown and crimson birds;
The plain extends to an escarpment lit
Softly as by a steady candle flame;

And then there is the great curve of the earth
And, after, you, whom two seas and a war
Divides.
                    The dust blows up. As long as those
Photographs poison my imagination
I shall not dare to catch my countenance
In any mirror; for it seems to me
Our faces, bodies – both of us – are dead.

THE GREEN HILLS OF AFRICA

The green, humped, wrinkled hills: with such a look
Of age (or youth) as to erect the hair.
They crouch above the ports or on the plain,
Beneath the matchless skies; are like a strange
Girl's shoulders suddenly against your hands.
What covers them so softly, vividly?
They break at the sea in a cliff, a mouth of red:
Upon the plain are unapproachable,
Furrowed and huge, dramatically lit.

And yet one cannot be surprised at what
The hills contain. The girls run up the slope,
Their oiled and shaven heads like caramels.
Behind, the village, with its corrugated
Iron, the wicked habit of the store.
The villagers cough, the sacking blows from the naked
Skin of a child, a white scum on his lips.
The youths come down in feathers from the peak.
And over all a massive frescoed sky.

The poisoner proceeds by tiny doses,
The victim weaker and weaker but uncomplaining.
Soon they will only dance for money, will
Discover more and more things can be sold.
What gods did you expect to find here, with
What healing powers? What subtle ways of life?
No, there is nothing but the forms and colours,
And the emotion brought from a world already
Dying of what starts to infect the hills.

(64)

THE GIRAFFES

I think before they saw me the giraffes
Were watching me. Over the golden grass,
The bush and ragged open tree of thorn,
From a grotesque height, under their lightish horns,
Their eyes were fixed on mine as I approached them.
The hills behind descended steeply: iron-
Coloured outcroppings of rock half covered by
Dull green and sepia vegetation, dry
And sunlit: and above, the piercing blue
Where clouds like islands lay or like swans flew.

Seen from those hills the scrubby plain is like
A large-scale map whose features have a look
Half menacing, half familiar, and across
Its brightness arms of shadow ceaselessly
Revolve. Like small forked twigs or insects move
Giraffes, upon the great map where they live.

When I went nearer, their long bovine tails
Flicked loosely, and deliberately they turned,
An undulation of dappled grey and brown,
And stood in profile with those curious planes
Of neck and sloping haunches. Just as when,
Quite motionless, they watched I never thought
Them moved by fear, a wish to be a tree,
So as they put more ground between us I
Saw evidence that these were animals
With no desire for intercourse, or no
Capacity.
                    Above the falling sun,
Like visible winds the clouds are streaked and spun,
And cold and dark now bring the image of
Those creatures walking without pain or love.

THE PLAINS

The only blossoms of the plains are black
And rubbery, the spiked spheres of the thorn,
And stuffed with ants. It is before the rains:
The stream is parched to pools, occasional
And green, where tortoise flop; the birds are songless;
Towers of whirling dust glide past like ghosts.
But in the brilliant sun, against the sky,
The river course is vivid and the grass
Flaxen: the strong striped haunches of the zebra,
The white fawn black, like flags, of the gazelles,
Move as emotions or as kindly actions.
The world is nothing but a fairy tale
Where everything is beautiful and good.

At night the stars were faint, the plateau chill;
The great herds gathered, were invisible,
And coughed and made inarticulate noises
Of fear and yearning: sounds of their many hooves
Came thudding quietly. The headlights caught
Eyes and the pallid racing forms. I thought
Of nothing but the word *humanity*:
And I was there outside the square of warmth,
In darkness, in the crowds and padding, crying.
Suddenly the creamy shafts of light
Revealed the lion. Slowly it swung its great
Maned head, then – loose, suède, yellow – loped away.
O purposeful and unapproachable!
Then later his repugnant hangers-on:
A pair of squint hyenas limping past.
This awful ceremony of the doomed, unknown
And innocent victim has its replicas
Embedded in our memories and in
Our history. The archetypal myths
Stirred in my mind.

> The next day, over all,
The sun was flooding and the sky rose tall.
Where rock had weathered through the soil I saw

A jackal running, barking, turning his head.
Four vultures sat upon the rock and pecked,
And when I neared them flew away on wings
Like hair. They left a purple scrap of skin.
Have I discovered all the plains can show?
The animals gallop, spring, are beautiful,
And at the end of every day is night.

ASKARI'S SONG

At dusk when the sky is pale,
Across a three years' journey
I can see the far white hill
Which in my land is like a
Conscience or maker.

At dusk when cattle cross
The red dust of the roadway,
I smell the sweetish grass,
Half animal, half flowers,
Which also is ours.

At dusk the roads along
The separating plains are
So sad with our deep song
I could expect the mountain
To drift like a fountain,

And, conquering time, our tribe
Out of the dust to meet us
Come happy, free, alive,
Bringing the snow-capped boulder
Over their shoulder.

THE WHITE CONSCRIPT AND
THE BLACK CONSCRIPT

I do not understand
Your language, nor you mine.
If we communicate
It is hardly the word that matters or the sign,
But what I can divine.

Are they in London white
Or black? How do you know,
Not speaking my tongue, the names
Of our tribes? It could be as easily a blow
As a match you give me now.

Under this moon which the curdled
Clouds permit often to shine
I can see more than your round cap,
Your tallness, great eyes and your aquiline
Nose, and the skin, light, fine.

The British must be wicked:
They fight. I have been brought
From our wide pastures, from
The formal rules of conduct I was taught;
Like a beast I have been caught.

If only I could tell you
That in my country there
Are millions as poor as you
And almost as unfree: if I could share
Our burdens of despair!

For I who seem so rich,
So free, so happy, am
Like you the most despised.
And I would not have had you come
As I most loath have come.

Among our tribe, like yours,
There are some bad, some good –
That is all I am able to say:
Because you would not believe me if I could
Tell you it is for you, the oppressed, the good
Only desire to die.

NATIVES WORKING ON THE
AERODROME

Curls powdered with chalk like a black roman bust,
This prisoner, convicted of a lust
For maize, is whipped to building a great shed
For bombers; and bears the earth upon his head.

THE TRIBES

I think of the tribes: the women prized for fatness
Immovable, and by a sympathetic
   Magic sustaining the herds,
   On whose strange humps sit birds;

And those with long dung-stiffened capes of hair,
And those that ceremonially eat their dead;
   The ornamental gashes
   Festered and raised with ashes;

The captured and dishonoured king compelled
To straddle a vertical and sharpened stake,
   Until, his legs hauled at,
   The point burst from his throat;

And all the prohibitions and the cheapness
Of life so hardly got, where it is death
   Even to touch the palace
   And poison expresses malice.

Now in the white men's towns the tribes are gathered
Among the corrugated iron and
    The refuse bins where rats
    Dispute with them for scraps.

Truly, civilisation is for them
The most elemental struggle for bread and love;
    For all the tabus have gone,
    It is man against man alone.

On waste plots and in the decrepit shanties
They begin to discover the individual,
    And, with the sense in time
    Of Adam, perpetuate crime.

The most horrible things you can imagine are
Happening in the towns and the most senseless:
    There are no kings or poison,
    Are laws but no more reason.

TEBA

He fled. The long deserted street,
Moonlit, the moon so mauve, so near,
The sound of his naked throbbing feet,
And, looking back, the body's clear
And indestructible shape of fear –
Now these are memories and dreams:
Again life is nearly as it seems.

Across the plains, the mountain, white
At dawn, the country's ghostly fold,
Rose up, he knew, from distant bright
Forests of home. He turned: the cold
Downs fell to grasses parched and gold,
Thorn trees and fissures, slim dun birds,
Vast startled wheeling racing herds.

These plains are endless: as the day
Deepened the mountain faded and
The corrugated air drew clay –
Hued whirls of dust across the bland
Sky; the skin stiffened on his hand.
He tracked a half-dry stream until
Exhaustion overcame his will.

A nightmare clawed his sleep: he was
Before remote pale men. 'Confess!'
'I am not guilty of this thing because
Kwa bade me – if a man possess
A shamba he may ask, no less,
His friend to dig it.' This he knew
Was folly. The judges said: 'Untrue.'

A lizard flaming from the sun
Flickered across his skin: his eyes
Opened: the lizard seemed his sin.
The dreams and the realities
Fused in his heart-proceeding sighs:
'I am that Teba who has killed
And who cannot kill the pursuing world.'

But in the fluid air of dusk,
Beyond the purpling plains there gleamed
Once more that summit, like a tusk.
So every dawn and evening seemed
To promise he should be redeemed,
Changing the world's for the tribe's rebuke,
The cold for the fond regretful look –

Until the heavens, huge and light,
At last were filled by mountain. He
Was home: his sable skin scratched white
And red was stretched above the valley,
The coins of thatch, the childhood tree,
The half-bared rocks the shade of sand
Where nightly oblique hyenas stand.

Still as though frozen by a wizard,
The village lay, while over it
And him the shadow that a buzzard
Throws ominously slowly beat.
Now it is not his pursuers sit
Upon him but the crushing weight
Of the intolerable too-late.

And some strange commerce starts between
The making and the man, the lack
Within, the rich without; the green
Mutation and the later black.
At length he saw upon the track,
Puffed in the windless air like fumes
Of acid, white and belligerent plumes –

A warrior that the chief had sent,
The many's message to the one,
So feminine and insolent
In look, his voice so deep in tone,
Whose trappings wakened Teba's own
Archaic past, the ritual
In which he once had played a rôle.

The warrior's words fell like a net:
Beneath the ochre Teba saw
The features that a boy might get.
The paint said: 'Teba, I am law.
I am the chief's voice and I know
You have committed murder which
Cannot be hidden in a ditch.'

Whispered the face behind the paint:
'My friend, I know you. We live by
A creeping shade which here is faint
But which eventually will dye
All with the blackness of a lie.
The plumes are shabby, the paint no longer
Impresses, our arms will not kill danger.'

(72)

But the official mask still said:
'Death, Teba, has no longer reasons;
For with the white king I have made
A treaty, and through all the seasons
Of man and nature death holds feasance
Only to death, and we have lost
The mastery of that which is last.

'Further, I have agreed to give
Some warriors for the white man's war –
Gave you who have no right to live.
Such warriors I sent to shore
That opening and fearful door
That lets destructive spectres in,
Efficient and barbarian.

'I cannot judge you, Teba, only
Command. You must return to death.'
The warrior went down: the lonely
Forest expired its evening breath
As Teba took the other path,
And night extended rapidly
From roots and vermin to the sky.

Having no other link but languor
With this familiar, poignant place,
He lay between the two worlds' danger
And slept. And woke to find a face,
Vivid and weird, against the lace
Of green upon the cobalt's fleeced
Horizon: saw it was the priest.

His features were of crumpled paper,
The pupils of the eyes were running
Into the whites. A ritual caper
Rattled the bangles, and the cunning
Mouth said: 'It is no use shunning
The world of men or trying to hide
From what is certainly inside.'

Cried Teba: 'But I am condemned!'
'Your body,' said the priest, 'may be
In peril of extinction, hemmed
By warring temporal powers, but we
Are not concerned with that. The free
Part of you that remains is ours,
Which needs our bandages and flowers.

'There is no remedy for that
Ulcer of guilt except the old
Ceremonies of our race, the great
Purification of the bold.'
Said Teba: 'I have learned to hold
Life dear from those who thought me black
And cheap. I cannot give it back.'

The priest crouched on his withered hams,
Removed his cap of horns, and said:
'Useless to go on with the forms
When what inside them is quite dead;
But even the very old crave bread,
And I must try to justify
My powers to society.

'Teba, no doubt I do forget
How to make rain. And you may think
My dress ridiculous. And yet
I brought you once across the brink
Of youth, and when your parents shrink
From things which round the dying press
It is to me they will confess.'

Sleepy, he mumbled: 'The result
Is certain, and the white man's coming
Perhaps was good: now we get salt.'
In a high voice he started humming,
His head swayed to phantasmal drumming;
And from him Teba crept as one
Who finds his father merely man.

He saw, across the river's steep
Channel, the cattle and the crop
And, as he had imagined – deep
Breasts tolling as she hacked the slope
Of rusty earth, her gleaming rope
Of back curved gently down – his wife,
And all the darkness of his life.

He hurried past his moving heart
To where the sidling river fell,
And thrust the tall green weeds apart
And sank in misery, with all
The nameless and impossible
Desires of those who prowl the grove,
In whose tongue is no word for love.

And through his fingers saw the clear
Water beside the dove-smooth stone;
Dragonflies, colourless with sheer
Speed, rest on grasses and regain
The chemical brilliance of a stain;
Green hands of cactus, arteries –
Unearthed by water – of the trees.

His spirit then leaped out to face
Victim and warrior, priest and wife,
The whole procession of his race,
And in that moment knew the knife
Descending on their ancient life,
That must make, of necessity,
An end, could start their history;

And summoned up his people, saw
How they converse and always gaze
At the angle of the speaking jaw
And never at each other's eyes;
And how the young men go their ways
Hand clasping hand; and how the old
Retain the innocence of the wild:

(75)

Saw the huge eyes of youth with that
Which in their glistening whites is like
Another iris probing at
The unseen with an eager look:
And arms escaping in a lake
From stuff, like softest leather, bright
With innumerable points of light.

Teba withdrew his hands: the sun
Gilded his view. And down the rocks
And on the flower-blue sky moved men
That made his world a closing box.
The guns clicked and the word that knocks
Against the heart. But Teba, fuller
Than fear, was filled with rising colour.

AUTUMN 1942

Season of rains: the horizon like an illness
Daily retreating and advancing: men
Swarming on aircraft: things that leave their den
And prowl the suburbs: cries in the starlit stillness

Into the times' confusion such sharp captions
Are swiftly cut, as symbols give themselves
To poets, though the convenient nymphs and elves
They know fall sadly short of their conceptions.

I see giraffes that lope, half snake, half steed,
A slowed-up film; the soft bright zebra race,
Unreal as rocking horses; and the face –
A solemn mandarin's – of the wildebeest.

And sometimes in the mess the men and their
Pathetic personal trash become detached
From what they move on; and my days are patched
With newspapers about the siege-like war.

Should I be asked to speak the truth, these are
What I should try to explain, and leave unsaid
Our legacy of failure from the dead,
The silent fate of our provincial star.

But what can be explained? The animals
Are what you make of them, are words, are visions,
And they for us are moving in dimensions
Impertinent to use or watch at all.

And of the men there's nothing to be said:
Only events, with which they wrestle, can
Transfigure them or make them other than
Things to be loved or hated and soon dead.

It is the news at which I hesitate,
That glares authentically between the bars
Of style and lies, and holds enough of fears
And history, and is not too remote.

And tells me that the age is thus: chokes back
My private suffering, the ghosts of nature
And of the mind: it says the human features
Are mutilated, have a dreadful lack.

It half convinces me that some great faculty,
Like hands, has been eternally lost and all
Our virtues now are the high and horrible
Ones of a streaming wound which heals in evil.

SADNESS, THEORY, GLASS

My poignant coffee does not last the twilight.
Gazing across the wide street through the central
Island of palms, I see the tight silk sky
As green as caterpillars, fretted by
The silhouettes of banks and consulates.

(77)

Cast up by war upon this neutral shore
I feel I should deliver a summing-up
Of all the passion, boredom, history,
Of all the suddenly important lives;
A rounded statement like Cézanne's of apples.
I wish I were as sure as he appears,
And wonder if the awful gaps in feeling,
Defects of seeing and experience,
Will vanish retrospectively, and this
Slight poetry, like a convex mirror, hold
A cosmos, lilliputian but exact.

I see the future like a theory –
The proof of pamphlets, as ordained erectness
After an age of stooping, or the knowledge
Of murderous glaciers in a million years.
The future is tomorrow, but today
I fold my blanket and that moment is
Immense: I walk across the airfield and
The aircraft, like stuffed birds, are there for ever,
Horrible to the touch. The present is
A lucid but distorting medium,
As though the cunning of perspective had
Been lost by nature and all was flat and wild
And terribly more truthful. Only the past
Is real, because it stays as sadness, like
Old age remembering sexually its youth.
There is no luxury of sentiment –
Simply regret, as those regret in bedlams
Their last concession to their mania.

But we shall reach at last the day of death
Or hear guns die seditiously to silence.
There is a time when on reality
The vision fits, and sadness, theory, glass,
Fuse, and the mass directs its destiny.
The integration is the action, I
Can only scribble on the margin: here
We saw strange southern stars revolve above

(78)

The struck ship swaying from the pointed convoy;
Here kitted-up for sun, here snow; and strangely
Realised here that out of all the world
Only one other in our life would know us.

WHAT IS TERRIBLE

Life at last I know is terrible:
The innocent scene, the innocent walls and light
And hills for me are like the cavities
Of surgery or dreams. The visible might
Vanish, for all it reassures, in white.

This apprehension has come slowly to me,
Like symptoms and bulletins of sickness. I
Must first be moved across two oceans, then
Bored, systematically and sickeningly,
In a place where war is news. And constantly

I must be threatened with what is certainly worse:
Peril and death, but no less boring. And
What else? Besides my fear, my misspent time,
My love, hurt and postponed, there is the hand
Moving the empty glove; the bland

Aspect of nothing disguised as something; that
Part of living incommunicable,
For which we try to find vague adequate
Images, and which, after all,
Is quite surprisingly communicable.

Because in the clear hard light of war the ghosts
Are seen to be suspended by wires, and in
The old house the attic is empty: and the furious
Inner existence of objects and even
Ourselves is largely a myth: and for the sin

To blame our fathers, to attribute vengeance
To the pursuing chorus, and to live
In a good and tenuous world of private values,
Is simply to lie when only truth can give
Continuation in time to bread and love.

For what is terrible is the obvious
Organization of life: the oiled black gun,
And what it cost, the destruction of Europe by
Its councils; the unending justification
Of that which cannot be justified, what is done.

The year, the month, the day, the minute, at war
Is terrible and my participation
And that of all the world is terrible.
My living now must bear the laceration
Of the herd, and always will. What's done

To me is done to many. I can see
No ghosts, but only the fearful actual
Lives of my comrades. If the empty whitish
Horror is ever to be flushed and real,
It must be for them and changed by them all.

A WRY SMILE

The mess is all asleep, my candle burns.
I hear the rain sharp on the iron roof
And dully on the broad leaves by the window.
Already someone moans, another turns
And, clear and startling, cries 'Tell me the truth'.

The candle throws my shadow on the wall
And gilds my books: tonight I'd like to bring
The poets from their safe and paper beds,
Show them my comrades and the silver pall
Over the airfield, ask them what they'd sing.

Not one of them has had to bear such shame,
Been tortured so constantly by government,
Has had to draw his life out when the age
Made happiness a revolution, fame
Exile, and death the whimsy of a sergeant.

But without envy I remember them,
And without pity look at my condition:
I give myself a wry smile in the mirror
– The poets get a quizzical ahem.
They reflect time, I am the very ticking:

No longer divided – the unhappy echo
Of a great fault in civilization; inadequate,
Perhaps, and sad, but strictly conscious no one
Anywhere can move, nothing occur,
Outside my perfect knowledge or my fate.

SHORE LEAVE LORRY

The gigantic mass, the hard material,
That entering our atmosphere is all
Consumed in an instant in a golden tail,
Is not more alien, nor the moon more pale:
The darkness, countries wide, where muscled beasts
Cannot link fold on fold of mountains, least
Mysterious: the stars are not so still.
Compared with what? In low gear up the hill
The lorry takes its load of strange wan faces,
Which gaze where the loping lion has his bases,
Like busts. Over half the sky a meteor falls;
The gears grind; somewhere a suffering creature calls.

UPON A REVOLUTIONARY KILLED
IN THE WAR

One who would not escape
If he could, the boredom and danger;
A theory had visible shape
In his life. No delight or anger
Lightened his course, and all
The things that could occurred.
Actions can only kill:
Let his epitaph be a word.

SPRING 1943

I

The skies contain still groves of silver clouds,
The land is low and level, and the buzzards
Rise from a dead and stiff hyena. Hazards
Of war and seas divide me from the crowds
Whose actions alone give numbers to the years;
But all my emotions in this savage place
This moment have a pale and hungry face:
The vision metropolitan appears.
And as I leave the crawling carcase, turning
Into the scrub, I think of rain upon
Factories and banks, the shoulders of a meeting:
And thoughts that always crouch in wait come burning –
Slim naked legs of fabulous and fleeting
Dancers, and rooms where everyone has gone.

II

Always it is to you my thoughts return
From harrowing speculation on the age,
As though our love and you were fictional
And could not ever burn as cities burn,
Nor die as millions, but upon a page
Rested delightful, moving and immortal.
This momentary vision fades. Again

You join the sheeted world whose possible death
Is also ours, and our nostalgic breath
Expires across two continents of pain.
And clearly I see the organizations of
The oppressed, their dangerous and tiny actions,
The problematic serum of the factions,
In these decayed and crucial times, as love.

III

Intelligent, fair and strictly moral as
A heroine of Jane's; here where the hill
Is in another country and shadows pass
Like towns, I think of you so civilized still.
And in that chaos of Europe which surrounds
Your little calm I see those leaping, rising,
Almost engendered by the times, the hounds
Of courage, hawks of vision, and the surprising
Gazelles of love. And so I run through all
The virtues, and this hopeless, barbarous space,
Which sometimes I think the future's self, can fall
Into its ancient and forgotten place.
No, I will not believe that human art
Can fail to make reality its heart.

WAR LETTERS

The letters are shockingly real,
Like the personal belongings
Of someone recently dead.

The letters are permanent,
And written with our hands,
Which crease into their lines

And breathe, but are not so
Living as these letters.
Our hands are seas apart;

A pair might cease to live
While the indestructible letter
Turned lies, flew to the other.

The letters express a love
We cannot realize:
Like a poignant glove

Surviving a well-known hand,
They can outlast our bodies
And our love transcend.

THE COAST

In the garden of the aerated water factory
Is an iron fountain and the doves
Come to its lip to drink.
Outside the totos are begging for five cent pieces;
Boys whose faces are done in sepia, the places
Round their eyes and the irises still running.
One of them is in the fifth class at the Government School:
He wants to be a teacher and tells me
That London is very cold.
This white town is at the mouth of a river
Which holds a star-shaped island;
And all the islands of the coast
Have satisfying shapes
As, flat and green, they float upon the water.
The palms make brittle noises in the wind;
At night they are prodigious plumes; among them
The sailing crescent moon glows,
And clouds which in the daytime would be white
Fume across the stars.
In the garden I think of things
For which these are inadequate images.
The white doves in the sunlight flutter in the blown
Spray from the fountain.
There is no substitute for the harsh and terrible
Facts of the time, which only longing

And sadness cloak,
And which have grown meaningless and commonplace.
My thoughts wander to the strong and desirable
Body of a girl shown as she arranged her blanket,
The swollen and fibrous, frightening leg of a beggar,
And on the road to the hospital
The bloody negro borne by his friends.
Round them stretch the lovely and legendary islands,
The jewel-coloured sea, and far,
Cold Europe.

NIGHT

It is the null part of the night,
And I am sick of some intense
Dissociation from the act
Of living, as I wake and fight
Dark with my eyes, and every sense
Slowly perceives its offered fact.

Here are the pillows and the bed,
And here my stretched-out limbs; here
Sharply are matches and a book, the mess,
And my ranged comrades like the dead,
Invisible but with their near
And incoherent presences.

Hamlet had more diseases than
His age, and felt them when the gun
Was silent and his mother sleeping,
His gnawing for Ophelia thin:
It was the terror in the sun;
His happy body's curious weeping.

I strike a match and reach the door –
Deep green and light-reflecting palms,
High clouds and the higher empty sky,
The chaos of stars, the unseen shore
Of all the islands, and the arms
Of sea, as brilliant as an eye:

And no dead in their millions, no
Burning or torture, no nightmarish
Slippings down the abyss of time
Backwards, but only, as long ago
He looked, man looking on the garish,
Struggling to find it the sublime.

Emotionless, the forms of nature
Confront the upright system of cells,
That ailing and inadequate
Machine, that nerve and flesh-racked creature,
Who from his spirit's endless hells
Made his reality and fate.

CRUSTACEANS

Upon the beach are thousands of crabs; they are
Small, with one foreclaw curiously developed.
Against the ashen sand I see a forest
Of waving, pink, in some way human, claws.
The crabs advance or, perhaps, retreat a step
And then like Hamlet's father slowly beckon
With that flesh-coloured, yes, obscene, incisor.
These actions in the mass take on a rhythm
– The sexual display of higher beasts,
The dance of the tribe, or the enthusiasm
Of a meeting.
                        If you go closer to the crabs
You see that with their normal claws they are making
Spheres from the sand, small perfect rounds, which they,
After a little preliminary twiddling,
Produce from beneath their bodies suddenly,
Like jugglers, and deposit by their holes.
While this goes on, that monstrous foreclaw, that
Button hole, is motionless. And all around
The shafts sunk by these creatures lie the eggs
Of sand, so patiently, endlessly evolved.

At last I stretch and wave my hand: the crabs
Instantly bolt down their holes and pull a sphere,
A trap door, after them, and in a second
The beach is still.

                  While I was watching them
My eyes unfocused with the effort, or
Maybe it was the whole activity
Which like an idea detached itself from its
Frame, background: and I thought, are these that I
Regard with such pity, disgust, absorption, crabs?

THE PETTY OFFICERS' MESS

Just now I visited the monkeys: they
Are captive near the mess. And so the day
Ends simply with a sudden darkness, while
Again across the palm trees, like a file,
    The rain swings from the bay.

The radio speaks, the lights attract the flies,
Above them and the rain our voices rise,
And somewhere from this hot and trivial place
As the news tells of death, with pleasant face,
    Comes that which is not lies.

The voices argue: *Soldiers in the end*
Turn scarecrows; their ambiguous figures blend
With all who are obsessed by food and peace.
The rulers go, they cannot order these
    Who are not disciplined.

O cars with abdicating princes: streets
Of untidy crowds: O terrible defeats!
Such images which haunt us of the past
Flash on the present like the exile's vast
    Shivers and fleshy heats;

But never coincide. Do they approach?
Upon that doubt I'm frightened to encroach –
Show me, I say, *the organizations that*
Will change the rags and mob into the state,
   Like pumpkin into coach.

The voices make no answer. Music now
Throbs through the room and I remember how
The little pickaxe shapes of swallows swerve
From balconies and whitewashed walls; a curve
   Of bird-blue bay; a dhow:

Small stabbing observations! And I know
(The cheap song says it on the radio)
That nerves and skin first suffer when we part,
The deep insensitive tissues of the heart
   Later, when time is slow.

And time has done his part and stands and looks
With dumb exasperated face. The books
Year after year record the crisis and
The passion, but no change. The measuring sand
   Is still. There are no flukes,

Like the virtuous sulphonamides, to kill
The poisons of the age, but only will:
Reduction of desires to that cold plan
Of raping the ideal; the new frail man
   Who slays what's in the hill.

The monkeys near the mess (where we all eat
And dream) I saw tonight select with neat
And brittle fingers dirty scraps, and fight,
And then look pensive in the fading light,
   And after pick their feet.

They are secured by straps about their slender
Waists, and the straps to chains. Most sad and tender,
They clasp each other and look round with eyes
Like ours at what their strange captivities
   Invisibly engender.

TODAY AND TOMORROW

Tomorrow let us drive between the hills
And visit our good friends upon the farms,
Walking among the rows of sugar cane
To look across their tassels at the snows.

And let us say good-day to sweet brown boys
Who keep their goats beneath that sheeted peak.
To morrow life will certainly be simple,
As at the drawing of an evening curtain.

Today there is the body to dispose of,
The blood to try to scour from all the house:
One must give lying smiles to calling neighbours
And soothe the children in the bedroom crying.

Today there is that terrible sense of guilt
And fear of being discovered; there is still
Regret for yesterday when everything
Was quiet and loving in tomorrow's way.

THE LEGIONS

When we have pissed away the marble walls,
And turned a foreign vandyke in the suns,
And lions wander in the ruined halls
And come and lick the barrels of our guns,
And the last letter has arrived and been
Forgotten, and the nights are dreamless –

                                        Then
Shall we be free? And turn for home, as lean
And baffled wolves turn for their starving den?
Or shall we merely look upon our nails
And see what kind of beasts we have become;
And weep at that: or, if our nature fails,
Shrug, and descend to dancing and the drum?

Exile has sores which battle cannot make,
Changing the sick from sound, the truth from fake.

(89)

SEPTEMBER 3, 1943

Does anyone believe in what appears –
Caught in the sights of rifles, or the flames
Blurring a city, rubble, deserts, tears,
Or photographs of statesmen, lists of names?
No; the rough years, their flotsam of events
And men and objects are to us unreal
Who have a secret, incoherent life
As deep as wrecks, and cannot think or feel:
But urge on and dissipate the hours that should
Be precious; gloat on the mounting dead; who know
There must be so much ill before the good.
So much. Oh fearful knowledge, that of time
Makes simply an unbearable suspense
Between the anniversaries of doom!

THE EMOTION OF FICTION

Reading a book of tales
Which has stirred my imagination,
I have put down the book
And stared at the congregation
Of shadows and hollows which then
Made up the world; and found
Such meaning in meaningless things –
The neutral, patterned ground,
The figures on the sky –
As made me ache to tell
The single secret that runs,
Like a tendon, through it all.
And I could promise then
An overwhelming word,
A final revelation –
The image of a seabird
With scimitars of wings,
Pathetic feet tucked away,
A fine, ill-omened name,
Sweeping across the grey.

And I knew then the purpose
Of everything; that illusion
That comes in the unexpected
Moment, an aimed explosion.
Perhaps the object of art
Is this: the communication
Of that which cannot be told.
Worse: the rich explanation
That there is nothing to tell;
Only the artificial
Plot and ambiguous word,
The forged but sacred missal.
Even the word becomes
Merely a path to meaning;
It is the plot that stays
Longest, a model of leaning
Out over raging seas,
As if our ship or longing
Could weather infinite water
Or fatal, ghostly thronging.
If one could invent a plot
Whose action was slow as life
But vivid and absorbing,
With a last twist of the knife,
Virtues of furious neatness,
Coincidence, surprise,
The loves of the old or plain
Made plausible as lies.
And all to be ideal,
Even the gross and stupid
Details of passion and death
That one can never decide
Whether nothing or everything –
And then? Would that be more
Precise than this intense
But vague emotion? Roar,
Lions of living flesh,
On bone-strewed plains! It is
The winged and semi-human
Monsters of civilised myths

Whose terrible questions, above
Familiar evil or good,
Are unanswerable, but
Whose tongue is understood.

THE STATUE

The noises of the harbour die, the smoke is petrified
Against the thick but vacant, fading light, and shadows slide
From under stone and iron, darkest now. The last birds glide.

Upon this black-boned, white-splashed, far receding vista of grey
Is an equestrian statue, by the ocean, trampling the day,
Its green bronze flaked like petals, catching night before the bay.

Distilled from some sad, endless, sordid period of time,
As from the language of disease might come a consummate rhyme,
It tries to impose its values on the port and on the lime –

The droppings that by chance and from an uncontrollable
And savage life have formed a patina upon the skull;
Abandoned, have blurred a bodied vision once thought spare but
        full –

On me, as authority recites to boys the names of queens.
Shall I be dazzled by the dynasties, the gules and greens,
The unbelievable art, and not recall their piteous means?

Last night I sailed upon that sea whose starting place is here,
Evaded the contraptions of the enemy, the mere
Dangers of water, saw the statue and the plinth appear.

Last night between the crowded, stifling decks I watched a man,
Smoking a big curved pipe, who contemplated his great wan
And dirty feet while minute after tedious minute ran –

This in the city now, whose floor is permanent and still,
Among the news of history and sense of an obscure will,
Is all the image I can summon up, my thought's rank kill;

(92)

As though there dominated this sea's threshold and this night
Not the raised hooves, the thick snake neck, the profile, and the
    might,
The wrought, eternal bronze, the dead protagonist, the fight,

But that unmoving, pale but living shape that drops no tears,
Ridiculous and haunting, which each epoch reappears,
And is what history is not. O love, O human fears!

RETURN

There is before the night,
For us, a foreign twilight.
The grey waves rise and splinter:
We voyage into winter.
Beyond the disc of sea
Stretches our northern country.
Our blood made thin by burning
And poison is returning.
Is it too late, too late,
For dreams to approximate?
Will the port be the same,
Or have another name:
The road, the house, the wife,
Only a spectral life?

WINTER IN CAMP

I

A three badge killick in the public bar
Voluptuously sups his beer. The girl
Behind the counter reads an early *Star*.
Suddenly from the radio is a whirl
Of classical emotion, and the drums
Precisely mark despair, the violin
Unending ferment. Some chrysanthemums
Outside the window, yellow, pale, burn thin.

Not only these strange winter flowers take on
In this dread air the meaning of a myth,
But all the common objects now have gone
Into the littoral which borders death.
The ancient sailor holds an unplumbed glass;
The girl is instantly a sculptured mass.

II

The music and the shadows in the dark
Cinema stir a huge, authentic feeling,
And, when the lights come on, the shabby ceiling,
The scarred green walls and seats confirm the stark
Contrast between the crust and infinite deeps.
I go to the canteen, ramshackle, warm,
And move among the poor anonymous swarm;
I am awake but everybody sleeps.

Outside: the moonlit fields, the cruel blue –
Which box another world; as that absurd
Material life of sonneteers contains
A second, utterly unlike, self-made,
And contradicting all experience
Except this rarest, fearfullest, most true.

III

The trees I thought so cold and black and bare
In the late afternoon sprung softest browns:
The rain had stopped, and through the perspex air
The low sun made the land as green as downs.
The country hovered on a neutral edge;
And I was startled by a startled bird
Fluttering among the bayonets of the hedge –
And this is the illusion of the word.

Beyond the word, the chosen images,
Painful and moving as they are, I feel
Unutterably the epoch's tragedies,

Beside which this scene's cruelties are real
But hopelessly inadequate; like the pities
Of living airmen borne above smashed cities.

IV

What we imagined tortuously and dreaded
Comes like a friend advancing from the dark;
The morning sheet emphatically is leaded
With news of cities gone – and left unread.
And even as I write this, overhead,
The bombers fly to Europe. As I write:
In this bare camp, in country like a park,
Where uniforms and rain make thick the night.

Who now this winter dreads and who imagines?
The years of war pile on our heads like lime,
And horrors grow impersonal as engines;
Nor can I think in discipline and slime.
Perhaps beside some blue and neutral lake
Another Lenin sorts the real from fake.

V

Day after day upon the concrete square,
Cargo for sinking iron, sweaty places,
The men assemble with their cold, cramped faces,
Then go, for me forever, into air.
Their minds are full of images of fear,
Unending lust, their bodies in the traces
Of conformation: and the brief time races.
How will they recognize the crucial year?

Now man must be political or die;
Nor is there really that alternative.
Correctly to be dedicated and to live
By chance, is what the species asks. The sky
Is smutted with migrating birds or ships;
The kiss of winter is with cracking lips.

(95)

VI

And everywhere is that enormous lie;
So obvious that it seems to be the truth:
Like the first moment of a conjurer's failure,
Or visions of love from waves of cheap perfume
In villages on Sunday afternoons.
It even penetrates this quiet room,
Where three men round a stove are talking.
'The strikers should be shot,' one says: his hand
A craftsman's, capable and rough. The second:
'Niggers and Jews I hate.' It is the squawking
Of an obscene and guiltless bird. They sit,
Free men, in prison. And the third: 'I hate
Nobody' – raising, to gesticulate,
His arm in navy with a gun on it.

VII

Defined, undazzling, paper thin, the sun
At dusk: the moon at morning with the ghastly
Brightness of violet or mere decay.
And what, unconscious, we have truly done
Is done, and there remains the girl, the gun –
Embedded, actual, in the staring day
Night's symbols almost overwhelm us. Lastly:
The world which suffers of these things subtraction.

For what is now our life is neither dreams
Nor their more intricate and sensual stuff,
But that which to posterity descends
As formulae and measurements; which seems
To diggers, tombs, to critics, words; enough
To change the rôle of horses, hump waste sands.

VIII

What does the robin whisper and the trees,
Expressive of wind and winter, round this coast,
The human flesh that might contain a ghost?

Only plain words like *oil* and *manganese*.
It is not that our sensibilities
Are dead: what moved and frightened in the past
Confronts us still; still we construct the vast
Network of space from small realities.

But now the rotten crimson robes are falling,
What shaped them seen as bones with common names.
Magic is smothered under bribes, concessions:
Nothing beside the war can be appalling.
The victims of the sacrificial games
Discerned no symbolism in the lions.

IX

My working-party hacks the grass, the tall
Tubers of summer rusty as the sickle.
In camp a season, these young men have all
A respite from the battle over nickel
– Or dynasties or rubber, anything
But what is mass-induced into their heads.
And while they work they sentimentally sing:
As credulously they will go to beds
As graves.

        Their weakness is the measure of
My own; their guilt my own inactive past;
Their stormy future mine, who wish that love
Could melt the guns, expropriate a caste.
How, when my only rank is consciousness,
Can I despise them, far less pity, bless?

EPITAPHS FOR SOLDIERS

I

Passing soldier stop and think
I was once as sad as you,
Saw in history a brink
More fearful than a bayonet's blue
– And left to what I thought but birds
The human message of these words.

II

Incredibly I lasted out a war,
Survived the unnatural, enormous danger
Of each enormous day. And so befell
A peril more enormous and still stranger:
The death by nature, chanceless, credible.

WINTER NIGHT

An owl is hooting in the grove,
The moonlight makes the night air mauve,
The trees are regular as crystals,
The thawing road shines black as pistols,
And muffled by the quiet snow
The wind is only felt to blow.
Dread bird that punctually calls!
Its sound inhuman strangely falls
Within the human scale; and I
Am forced to place, besides the cry
The moon, the trees, the swollen snow,
Reluctantly with what I know.
Even the road conveys the sense
Of being outside experience;
As though, this winter night of war,
The world we made were mine no more.

DURING A BOMBARDMENT BY
V-WEAPONS

The little noises of the house:
Drippings between the slates and ceiling;
From the electric fire's cooling,
Tickings; the dry feet of a mouse:

These at the ending of a war
Have power to alarm me more
Than the ridiculous detonations
Outside the gently coughing curtains.

And, love, I see your pallor bears
A far more pointed threat than steel.
Now all the permanent and real
Furies are settling in upstairs.

EPILOGUE

No day seems final but there must be one
When death completes what was fragmentary,
And makes a symbol from futility,
As when the curtain falls, the audience gone,
There is a meaning though was purposed none.

And even all the war-lopped lives that we
Find so grotesque have, as the prowling sea
Or bullet comes to them, a satisfaction;
Dying they turn in retrospect to art.

So in our time all art seems meaningless,
Confused with life as brain might change to heart:
Who would invent when he as well might guess?

And where the pattern in the whole when part
Is virtuous, pitiful, complete, no less?

The little noises of the house:
Dropping between the slates and ceiling;
From the electric fire's cooling,
Ticking the dry tent of a mouse;

Then at the ending of a war
Have power to alarm me more
Than the ridiculous detonations
Outside the gently coughing curtains.

And, love, I see your pallor bear
A far more pointed threat than steel:
Now all the permanent and real
Furies are settling in upstairs.

EPILOGUE

No day seems final but the ultimate be one
When death completes what was fragmentary,
And makes a symbol from futility;
As when the curtain falls, the audience gone,
There is a meaning though was purposed none.

And even all the unwatched-dropped lives, that we
Find so grotesque alive, as the prowling sea
Or bullet can, so cheap, a satisfaction,
Dying they turn in retrospect to art.

So in our lives all art is meaningless,
Confused with life; as pain might change to heart?
Who should invent when life as well might guess?

And where the pattern in the whole when part
Is various, pitiful, complete, no less?

IV

VI

DEDICATORY EPISTLE, WITH A BOOK OF 1949

To Jack Clark and Alan Ross

Here's proof – as if one needed any –
Of Fuller's classic parsimony.
One volume, two dedicatees;
So little verse and less to please.
Alan, I hear you say, behind
That manner which is always kind:
'No meat, and where's the bloody gravy?
He wrote much better in the Navy'.
And you, Jack, glancing up from Proust:
'It's compromise come home to roost'.

Hysteria is the destiny
Of those who want, insatiably,
In childhood love; and the condition
Of being wet in bed's ambition.
What kind of pasts must we have led
That now we're neither red nor dead?
We had our fill of love and hunger
When uninhibited and younger:
After we lost the initial breast
We knew a falling off of zest;
And while the workless topped three million
Read Eliot in the pavilion;
For us the Reichstag burned to tones
Of Bach on hand-made gramophones;
We saw the long-drawn fascist trauma
In terms of the poetic drama;
And even the ensuing war
For most was something of a bore.

Dear Clark, it's you to whom I speak,
As one who hovered in that clique:
A wit and cause of wit in others;
Who called the working-class half-brothers;

Easy at Lords or Wigmore Hall;
A nibbler at the off-side ball –
We would have moved, were held, alas,
In the paralysis of class.
We spoke our thoughts not loud and bold
But whispered through the coward's cold;
And all the time, with deadly humour,
Inside us grew the traitor's tumour.
Nothing I say can warn, console,
You who've survived the liberal rôle,
And in a world of Camps and Bomb
Wait for the end with false aplomb.

The nineteenth century dream of good
Erecting barricades of wood
And storming keypoints of reaction
To substitute its kindly faction,
Until what's violent and rotten
Withers like warts tied round with cotton –
Such vision fades, and yet our age
Need not become the last blank page,
And though the future may be odd
We shouldn't let it rest with God;
Confused and wrong though things have gone
There is a side we can be on:
Distaste for lasting bread and peace
May thus support a king in Greece,
And trust in General Chiang Kai-shek
Will safely lead to freedom's wreck.

Our dreams no longer guard our sleep:
The noses of the road-drills creep,
With thoughts of death, across the lawn
Out of the swarthy urban dawn.
And one by one, against our will,
The cultured cities vanish till
We see with horror just ahead
The sudden end of history's thread.
Ross, with your innings' lead of years,
Such brooding will not bring your tears.

You lived when doom was not the fashion,
What's sad for you is human passion.
Your verse is sensuous, not spare,
Somerset in, not Lancashire.
We disagree in much, I know:
I'm over-fond of Uncle Joe;
You find in Auden not an era –
Simply a poet who grows queerer;
The working class for you's a fact,
No statue in the final act.
Yet we should never come to blows
On this – that man as artist goes,
And in that rôle, most sane, most free,
Fulfils his spacious infancy;
That truth's half feeling and half style,
And feeling and no style is vile.
About us lie our elder writers,
Small, gritty, barren, like detritus:
Resistance to the epoch's rage
Has not survived their middle age.
The type of ivory tower varies
But all live in the caves of caries.
The younger men, not long from mother,
Write articles about each other,
Examining, in solemn chorus,
Ten poems or a brace of stories.
The treason of the clerks is when
They make a fetish of the pen,
Forget that art has duties to –
As well as to the 'I' – the 'You',
And that its source must always be
What presses most, most constantly.
Since Sarajevo there has been
Only one thing the world could mean,
And each successive crisis shows
That meaning plainer than a nose.
Sassoon found Georgian style napoo
To state what he was going through:
And Owen knew why he was born –
To write the truth and thus to warn.

The poet now must put verse back
Time and again upon the track
That first was cut by Wordsworth when
He said that verse was meant for men,
And ought to speak on all occasions
In language which has no evasions.

Dear friends, I wish this book bore out
More than the bourgeois' fear and doubt.
Alas, my talent and my way
Of life are useless for today.
I might have cut a better figure
When peace was longer, incomes bigger.
The 'nineties would have seen me thrive,
Dyspeptic, bookish, half-alive.
Even between the wars I might
With luck have written something bright.
But now, I feel, the 'thirties gone,
The dim light's out that could have shone.
My richest ambiguity
Is nightmares now, not poetry:
After eight lines the latter ends
Unless I'm babbling to my friends.
The arteries and treaties harden,
The shadow falls across the garden,
And down the tunnel of the years
The spectre that we feared appears.
Gazing upon our love or book,
Between the lines or in the look,
We see that choice must fall at last,
And the immortal, lucky past –
Thinking of bed or lying in it –
Cry out and crumble in a minute.
For such times are these poems meant,
A muted, sparse accompaniment,
Until the Wagner we await
Provides a score that's up to date,
And world and way and godheads pass
To vulgar but triumphant brass.

ON SEEING THE LENI RIEFENSTAHL
FILM OF THE 1936 OLYMPIC GAMES

The nation's face above the human shape,
Sunlight on leaf, gloved skin and water pearled
– No art can hide the shocking gulfs that gape
Even between such bodies and their world.

Art merely lets these tenants of a star
Run once again with legendary ease
Across the screen and years towards that war
Which lay in wait for them like a disease.

ON HEARING BARTOK'S CONCERTO
FOR ORCHESTRA

Instinct with the division of labour peals
The sonorous and manufactured brass:
The lonely instrument and player caught
    And transcended by the mass.

At such art in our time one cannot help
But think with love and terror of the double
Man, and the puzzling dumb notation under
    Floors of the future's rubble.

SCHWERE GUSTAV

Schwere Gustav, built by Krupps,
Was the largest of all guns:
Of thirty-one-inch calibre,
It fired a shell of seven tons.

Worked by fifteen hundred troops
Topped by a general, no less,
Gustav fired two rounds a day,
But after sixty was u/s.

The soldiers seeing Gustav's barrel
Huge against the eastern sky,
And his complicated breech,
Knew why they had got to die.

Accumulated capital
Made possible this symbol of
Our deep, ridiculous desires.
O war, O Gustav and O love!

FATHERS AND SONS

Their sons, grown-up, the spectres lay;
The house is still again and light.
And then to war were marched away
Their sons, grown-up. The spectres lay.
The sons return: once more the grey
Figures make terrible the night.
Their sons, grown-up, the spectres lay:
The house is still again and light.

THE DIVIDED LIFE RE-LIVED

Once again the light refracted through the dusty crimson air
Leaves the spaces of the evening blurred and bare.
Bats that flicker round the edges of the square Victorian lawn
Symbolise the bourgeois souls from life withdrawn.

Now the nightingale arouses us upon the withered tree
With its disappointing, moving melody,
And against the chalky purple thrown by distant main-road arcs
Flow the tired suburban leaves like mouldy sparks.

Here the mower furred with grass like filings round a magnet's pole,
Teacups left for ants to make our fortunes droll;
While we sit and try to think that everything is not too late –
Sparrows sitting on the sad outfield of fate.

Once and only once we were in touch with brutal, bloody life
When we got in or kept out of global strife;
And in desert or in dockyard met our coarser fellow men,
Wielding friendly gun or scrubber, not our pen.

How we innocently thought that we should be alone no more,
Linked in death or revolution as in war.
How completely we have slipped into the same old world of cod,
Our companions Henry James or cats or God.

Waiting for the evening as the time of passion and of verse,
Vainly hoping that at both we shan't get worse:
While outside the demon scientists and rulers of the land
Pile the bombs like busy crabs pile balls of sand.

And the best that we can wish for is that still the moon will rise
Enigmatic, cracked and yellow to men's eyes,
And illuminate the manuscripts of poems that foretold
All the ruin and survival of the old.

MEDITATION

Now the ambassadors have gone, refusing
Our gifts, treaties, anger, compliance;
And in their place the winter has arrived,
Icing the culture-bearing water.
We brood in our respective empires on
The words we might have said which would have breached
The Chinese wall round our superfluous love
And manufactures. We do not brood too deeply.
There are our friends' perpetual, subtle demands
For understanding: visits to those who claim
To show us what is meant by death,
And therefore life, our short and puzzling lives,
And to explain our feelings when we look
Through the dark sky to other lighted worlds –
The well-shaved owners of sanatoria,

And raving, grubby oracles: the books
On diet, posture, prayer and aspirin art:
The claims of frightful weapons to be investigated:
Mad generals to be promoted: and
Our private gulfs to slither down in bed.

Perhaps in spring the ambassadors will return.
Before then we shall find perhaps that bombs,
Books, people, planets, worry, even our wives,
Are not at all important. Perhaps
The preposterous fishing-line tangle of undesired
Human existence will suddenly unravel
Before some staggering equation
Or mystic experience, and God be released
From the moral particle or blue-lit room.
Or, better still, perhaps we shall, before
Anything really happens, be safely dead.

STANZAS

In the year's autumnal rage
When nations and leaves are rank
And with great tenderness
Horses stand head to flank,
Motionless under stress,
Upon their plinth of green,
I burrow through my age
To the cause of what has been.

The cause of what has been
Is fixed in the sensual past.
It was then that the deed or thought
Fulfilling the pattern was cast.
But the memory that ought
To give release from guilt
Hides in the stone ravine
That culture and time have built.

Culture and time have built
Their state upon a flaw:
The anguished faces gaze
From cold, symmetrical law.
And the happy beasts still graze
In their instinctive wood
Who have never plunged to the hilt
In their prince and father's blood.

Their prince and father's blood
In trivial, terrible guise
Returns to ferocious youth.
The sane cannot recognize
Their dreams, nor the mad the truth.
And into darkness the age
Whirls its pathetic good
In the year's autumnal rage.

1948

Reading among the crumbs of leaves upon
The lawn, beneath the thin October sun,
I hear behind the words
And noise of birds
The drumming aircraft; and am blind till they have gone.

The feeling that they give is now no more
That of the time when we had not reached war:
It is as though the lease
Of crumbling peace
Had run already and that life was as before.

For this is not the cancer or the scream,
A grotesque interlude, but what will seem
On waking to us all
Most natural –
The gnawed incredible existence of a dream.

VIRTUE

In these old hackneyed melodies
Hollow in the piano's cage
I see the whole trash of the age –
Art, gadgets, bombs and lies.

Such tunes can move me to confess
The trash moves, too: that what offends
Or kills can in its simplest ends,
Being human, also bless.

EPITAPH

Whoever you may be,
Killed by the times or time,
Lie underneath this rhyme
And feed the berried tree.
We cannot outlast verse
And verse lives best on this.
But stone can split. No worse
Chance of continuance is
The change to vegetable,
Immortal on the rubble.

THE LAKE

Once more the meditative poem. Léman,
Its peacock and its turquoise in the shapes
Of birthmarks, laps the shore where all the famous
Wrote in a storm of sails and alps and grapes.

The French side lifts its dark and green-pored face:
The train runs through the terraces to war:
Northwards the weather speaks: only upon
This sunlit hub is reason any more.

I think how force political, exerted
Across the squares and diamonds of states,
Gradually drove the masters to a corner
In which the single thought was human fate.

Rousseau and Gibbon found in history
And love some freedom yet of personal will:
And next the marching clock-arm swept the blue
On Shelley, and pushed Byron further still.

Then action ended: there was merely sadness –
Arnold returning to a *fait accompli*.
Around the lake the world fell twice in ruins.
The lake became anachronistic simply.

The trunks of plane trees dappled like giraffes;
The six blurred cygnets and the crystal swans;
The ancient gravel; peaks that float at night,
Veined with the peach of blood their skeletons;

Lizards, damp lashes, on the sun-dry stone;
Beyond the morning blinds the swallows shrieking
Like silk in skeins; the steamer's innocent missions –
Of these it is quite pointless to be speaking.

For all the symbols which the poets used
While the fires quivered and the needle turned,
Have lost their aliases, and can be uttered
Here only, where the century has not burned.

Perhaps there are new tropes for our own world
Where, in their madmen's stupor, empires wait,
The flies of factions on their rigid masks,
Lost in a dream of homicide and fate.

I do not know. I feel the lake preserved
For some new Gibbon's mildly-stirred repose,
In which, long after, lake-bound, he translates
Our frightful end to ornamental prose.

KNOLE

Inside the sombre walls the neat quadrangles still are green
As though a light shone on them from a sun, grey-masked, unseen.

And some remoter light leans through the embrasures of the house
And frees the colours of the hangings – crimson, lime and mouse.

The firedogs dangerous weapons, beds tents, rooms an insect's maze,
But nothing burns, loves, spies, through rain- or history-nervous days.

An ancient painted Sackville down the chamber from the frame
Looks over what has lost its meaning yet is still the same.

He stares and will stare pointlessly, stiff in his mint brocades,
Hair reddish, bearded, white of hand, until our living fades.

His face the worried, capable, Elizabethan face,
He stands with the fresh-created ruler's half self-conscious grace.

Of savagery, the codpiece in the fairy's clothes remains;
All else the civilizing new discovery of gain.

Vestigial organs in their jars his stuffs and filigree:
The capital he started now explodes spontaneously.

But still outside, upon the deer-striped lawns, the trees are caught
Spread in the sheltering crystal of the mansion's stored-up thought;

And like those dreams of treasure only stir to accumulate
Their golden leaves in natural rhythms, endless, sad, sedate.

In this calm magic island in tempestuous seas, the plan
Holds yet: the spirits of earth and air still serve the passionate man.

CHEKHOV

Chekhov saw life as a series of departures;
Its crises blurred by train times, bags, galoshes.
Instead of saying the important word
The hurried characters only breathe Farewell.

And what there was of meaning in it all
Is left entirely to the minor figures:
Aged or stupid, across the deserted stage,
They carry, like a tray, the forgotten symbol.

EMILY DICKINSON

A few old props, a few new words –
    The drama breathes again:
And in the parlour, on the lawn,
    Blood ambles from its den.

The simple, solitary life
    Imagining, feeling all,
Postures and dabbles in the red
    Behind the bedroom wall.

And from those withered lips there come
    The world-deceiving cries:
'Love has no need of flesh'. 'The soul
    Perceives eternities'.

POETS

Of course, it's not a demon which possesses
Poets at that wild moment when the verse
Admits the saved-up image like a purse.
It is the id which has arranged its cesses
So as to season the prim ego's guesses.
Whether the thing goes better then or worse
Depends upon the gift or on the curse,
The poet's public life and private messes.
What wonder then that in the authentic go –
Romantic woolly hit or austere miss:
Running on nylon legs or broken castors –
Is some huge ambiguity, as though
The last line of a poem such as this
Were dead gold leaves against the garish asters.

EPITAPH FOR A SPY

Because his infancy was fixed on prying
His fated choice of a career was spying:
And so what father threatened was fulfilled –
The curiosity for secrets killed.

THE HERO

When the hero's task was done
And the beast lay underground,
In the time that he had won
From the fates that pushed him round

He had space to contemplate
How the peasants still were bled
And that in the salvaged state
Worms continued at the head.

Little space: already, where
Sweetly he enjoyed his fish,
Seeing through the shouldered hair
Loosening sails and dirty dish,

Gasped a pale new plea for aid.
Cleaning his gun later, he
Felt with awe the old beast's shade
Fall across the wine-dark sea.

IMAGE AND FOSSIL

The infant innocently thinks the adult free from error,
Free from anxiety and in the dark without his terror.

The father wonders how the son can break the imprisoning pattern
Of cells that over generations stretch unaltered, slattern.

The ageing poet thinks: 'Shall I continue to find strange themes?'
As he removes himself from action and dissects his dreams.

The civilization which observes its fatal symptoms asks:
'When I am gone will the barbarians set themselves my tasks?'

Through ice-ages of space the dubious particles move on,
Till the round destinies rise in them, brilliant, one by one.

Image and fossil undefeated lie among the lives
That fell in tragedy or plain despair upon their knives.

To worlds undreamt of in the shrinking orbit of our fears
Fly and take root like vivid grass the marvellous careers.

THE EXTENDING SEGMENT

Returning from the dead-end of my age,
The bones' revolt, the mind's dull rage,

I met that man enamoured of the state,
Whose healing powers were all too late.

And then the passionate youth who looked for love
But only found a mirrored dove.

And back still further to that murderous boy
Whose wish and principle was joy.

And yet I had not come to what had tangled
The strands that later they were mangled.

For that I must peer through my birth and see
The lines slope to infinity.

Enclosing in their segment all of nature
That separated man from creature:

Forbears who guarded from calamity
Seeds, love, and private imagery:

The murder of each stiff, dull generation
By its son's passionate revolution.

THE FIVE HAMLETS

The murdered king was Hamlet, and his spectre.
Hamlet, the son, a copy of the dead.
The sacrifice, foreteller and protector;
Dragon and guilt and hero in one head.

But this was only art: my child I called
Hamlet, who breathed and clung about his mother,
Remembering that former son, appalled,
Who saw his darling taken by another.

For I am that real Hamlet who endured,
And gave his rival all for which he burned;
Whose love collapsed in wrinkles, though uncured;
Whose ghost returned, returned, returned, returned.

ANCESTORS

The child enquires about his ancestors
    And looks from one stem to the other.
His questions make me gaze beyond the now
That trembles in the frailty of his mother.

And more: behind my self, compact, I see
    Irrelevant creatures of the past –
Giants of childhood, portraits on the wall,
Those of whom once I thought I was the last.

This bone-hard flesh I feel, the mind I use,
    Stretch over ages like a trope,
And face and feeling die and reappear
Till time has worn them perfect for my scope.

What I am like's an island, gnawed and drenched,
    Whose long root through the flux preserves;
With nose as dreaded, steered-for promontory,
And culture hanging on its mineral nerves.

So to the boy this haunted shade replies:
    Your ancestors were like you but grotesque:
Few are remembered, though to make you all
Feared for their sons, wrote verses at a desk.

LITTLE FABLE

The mouse like halting clockwork, in the light
A shade of biscuit, curved towards the right

And hid behind the gas stove, peeping out
A sickly moment with its pencil snout.

Its run was blocked to keep it in the wall
But at the time it was not there at all.

The food is covered and a penny trap,
Being bought, is baited with a bacon scrap.

Its back is guillotined and seen to be
Grey and not brown, its feet formed properly.

Thus the obscene becomes pathetic and
What mind had feared is stroked by hand.

THE FAMILY CAT

This cat was bought upon the day
That marked the Japanese defeat;
He was anonymous and gay,
But timorous and not discreet.

Although three years have gone, he shows
Fresh sides of his uneven mind:
To us – fond, lenient – he grows
Still more eccentric and defined.

(119)

He is a grey, white-chested cat,
And barred with black along the grey;
Not large, and the reverse of fat,
His profile good from either way.

The poet buys especial fish,
Which is made ready by his wife;
The poet's son holds out the dish:
They thus maintain the creature's life.

It's not his anniversary
Alone that's his significance:
In any case mortality
May not be thought of in his presence.

For brief as are our lives, more brief
Exist. Our stroking hides the bones,
Which none the less cry out in grief
Beneath the mocking, loving tones.

TO MY SON

When you can read and understand
This endless paper that I cover,
With what strange feeling will you find
That I, too, feared and loved, was sensitive, not clever.

For it is you to whom I write
(My only true posterity)
This verse that cannot better what
I seized from my environment and ancestry.

Dear boy, I should not mind your smile
At all the crudities and gaps,
Knowing thereby you could not fail
To build yourself across my craft and living's lapse.

The critic and the art in one;
Not tied by fate and yet unfree;
The classic killer, loving son;
Yes, you will know each word I add is irony.

THE GAZE

Catching myself obliquely in the glass,
I thought I saw my father.
He died at my age now, but the years that pass
Do not destroy him – rather
Make him resume his dense forgotten mass.

Although the memory of his face has gone
I know mine different,
And what I see in mirrors is the wan
Dwarf that the orbit bent –
The Dog-star's mysterious companion.

How well I understand what he transmitted!
The gaze that travelling
At will through the generations sees the pitted
Mask of the timeless thing,
And knows itself both weak and dedicated.

SLEEPING AND WAKING

I

I saw her tiny figure at the end
Of that enormous, bare room of my dream.
During the swift but hours-long journey, penned
To one thought and one look, there did not seem

Another life to which this was the key.
Desire was of intolerable weight
And tenderness beneath the anxiety
That she would go and I should be too late.

Her slender back towards me slowly grew
Into the copy of reality.
But then instead of that clear face I knew
She turned the future's sunken anguished lie.

Waking or sleeping now I see no more
What we imagined, only what we are.

My sleep stopped like a play. The lights came on,
And there was only normal life again:
The first birds tapping at the lawn, the rain
Still mottled on the glass. The shapes had gone
That woke me with their mimic of the past,
And showed too real for consciousness the meaning
Which, by the unremembered act and leaning
Wish, is upon the ambiguous present cast.

And yet the terror stayed. Inside these walls,
And coloured by the livid wash of dawn,
The darling sleepers copied death. I lay
Beside them, like an aeronaut who falls
To worse from danger, till the drapes were drawn
Upon the safe caged savagery of day.

BALLAD

Father, through the dark that parts us,
Through the howling winds I hear,
Come and drive away this dabbled
Ghost I fear.

But I've crossed the dark already
And am part of all you hear,
I shall never leave you, darling,
Do not fear.

NURSERY RHYME

Than the outlook of the ulcer
Nothing could be falser,
And the way of living of
The psychosis is not love.

In the good society
Morbid art's not necessary.
It's a sick subhuman voice
Comes from Kafka, Proust and Joyce.

After much analysis
Freud found he could not tell lies.
But in most there is no truth
After the initial tooth.

Though among both poor and rich
Are found the bully and the bitch,
Only those who haven't got
Can be free of what they've not.

Round the massive legs of man
Scuttle all the little men,
Busy planning for what's great
Their own ludicrous charred fate.

SONG

The blonde who reads *Prediction*,
The curate who reads Marx,
The poet who writes fiction,
The dog-lover who barks,
The dying who feel better,
The girl who buys quinine,
The wrist inside the fetter,
The bed behind the screen;

To such the ultimatum,
The test-tube in the rack,
The advertised pomatum,
The weakness of the back,
The psychopathic leader,
The laisser-faire of God,
The parent who's a bleeder,
The sergeant who's a sod,

Provide a normal setting
For runners in an age
Where life's not in the betting
And love's not on the stage,
Where there's no neat solution
For melting wills or gold,
And hope is revolution
And revolution's sold.

HYMN

Tell us how we can arrive at
Secrets locked behind the veil –
Byron's foot and James's privates,
Why Pope was pale.

Why we cannot still recall
What we did in bed with father –
Or what nurse said through the wall,
If you'd rather.

Put us in the way of knowing
Why we work our hair to toupees,
While the idle rich are flowing
In drop-head coupés.

Tell us why we wish for peace
While our nation swells its forces,
Why in others lust to crease
Us madly courses.

Now from all the ghastly land
Rise the swirling tea-leaves of
Rooks, and syphilitic stand
Stone boys of love.

Over bile-hued fields of May
Shines the day-time moon, a bone,
From them in this sad today
A light has flown.

While the leaders point, enraged,
And their people groan like ice,
Quietly sit the mad, engaged
With phantom lice.

Teach us thus to live in patience,
If you cannot teach us more,
Till progressive cerebration
Stops with war.

THE CIVILIZATION

By their frock-coated leaders,
By the frequency of their wars,
By the depth of their hunger,
Their numberless refugees,
And the brevity of their verse,
They were distinguished.

Their revolutions
Were thwarted by kisses.
The cold mathematicians
Aged into blurred philosophers.
Their poets choked on
The parallel of past calamities.

Their funeral customs, art,
Physique, and secret
Societies, unequal:
Their doom inevitable.
Ambiguous as dreams
Their symbolic poetry.

Yes, it had happened
Before. Ill-pictured leaders,
Food-queues in foodless places,
Migration to areas
Of moderate terror,
Monotonous poems.

Then horses galloping
Over burned foundations,
Ascetic communities,
The improbable moon,
Death from a cut,
Bleak, eroded spaces;

And eventually the strangers,
With the luxury of spices,
Effective weapons,
Their tales of travel,
Their ikons of leaders,
Their epic verse.

OBITUARY OF R. FULLER

We note the death, with small regret,
Of one who'd scarcely lived, as yet.
Born just before the First World War,
Died when there'd only been one more:
Between, his life had all been spent
In the small-bourgeois element,
Sheltered from poverty and hurt,
From passion, tragedy and dirt.
His infant traumas somewhat worse,
He would have written better verse,
His youth by prudence not so guided
His politics been more decided.
In the event his life was split
And half was lost bewailing it:
Part managerial, part poetic –
Hard to decide the more pathetic.
Avoiding China, Spain and Greece,
He passed his adult years of peace
In safe unease, with thoughts of doom
(As birth is feared inside the womb) –
Doom of his talent and his place,
Doom, total, of the human race.
This strange concern for fellow creatures

Had certainly some pathic features.
He could not understand that death
Must be the lot of all with breath,
And crudely linked felicity
With dying from senile decay,
Finding no spiritual worth
In guided missiles, torture, dearth.
Quite often he was heard to babble
'Poets should be intelligible'
Or 'What determines human fate
Is the class structure of the state'
Or 'Freud and Marx and Dickens found —
And so do I — souls not profound'.
These views were logically a feature
Of his rude, egotistic nature —
So unemotional and shy
Such friends as he retained would cry
With baffled boredom, thankful they
Were not part of his family.

If any bit of him survives
It will be that verse which contrives
To speak in private symbols for
The peaceful caught in public war.
For there his wavering faith in man
Wavers around some sort of plan,
And though foreseeing years of trouble,
Denies a universal rubble,
Discovering in wog and sailor
The presages of bourgeois failure.
Whether at this we weep or laugh
It makes a generous epitaph.

TAILPIECE

Emerging from the labour of the book —
The features fall together in a look,
And, shocked, one sees what was not there intended:
The wicked lover with the smug wife blended.

Epoch, speak not too unintelligibly
Through the cleft-palate: ambiguity
Of stance, cast some of that heroic shade
War and uprising have of living made.

And let the poetry be soon forgotten
In which the human animal seems rotten.
But, time, keep through whatever wretched ages
May be in store, the few courageous pages.

Reader, remember that behind the worst
There was of all resolves the writer's first,
The one neglected for its imagery –
To be as truthful as reality.

V

V

RHETORIC OF A JOURNEY

The train takes me away from the northern valleys
Where I lived my youth and where my youth lives on
In the person of my parent and the stone walls,
The dialect of love I understand
But scarcely speak, the mills and illnesses.

In Trollope's novel open on my knee
The characters are worried about money:
The action revolves round the right to a necklace.
I have only to bend my head and immediately
I am lost in this other reality, the world
Of art, where something is always missing.
In *The Eustace Diamonds* life is made tolerable
By standing away from time and refusing to write
Of the hours that link the official biography.

I think of the poem I wrote on another visit –
A list of the poet's hoarded perceptions:
The net of walls thrown over waves of green,
The valleys clogged with villages, the cattle
Pink against smoking mills – and only now
Experience what was delayed and omitted.
For those were rooms in which we dared not look
At each other's load of emotion: it was there
Our past had to die: and where we acknowledged
With pain and surprise our ties with the disregarded.
I would like to renounce the waking rational life,
The neat completed work, as being quite
Absurd and cowardly; and leave to posterity
The words on book-marks, enigmatic notes,
Thoughts before sleep, the vague unwritten verse
On people, on the city to which I travel.
I would like to resolve to live fully
In the barbarous world of sympathy and fear.

Says his life to the poet: 'Can you make verse of this?'
And the poet answers: 'Yes, it is your limitations
That enable me to get you down at all.'
The diamonds glitter on his paper and

His sons sail unloved to the Antipodes.
Those whom a lack of creativeness condemns
To truth see magazines in the hands of the patient
And realise that the serial will go on
After death; but the artist becomes ill himself.
For only the fully-committed participate
In the revolution of living, the coming to power
Of death: the others have always some excuse
To be absent from the shooting, to be at home
Curled up with a book or at the dentist's.

Sometimes I find it possible to feign
The accent of the past, the vulgar speech
Which snobbery and art have iced; but feel no longer
The compulsion of hills, the eternal interests
Which made my fathers understand each other.
That mockery of solidarity
Some of the civilised always experience,
Waiting half hopefully for the dreaded barbarians,
Sick of their culture, traitors to the division
Of toil and sensibility. Yet really
I can speak easily only to myself.
The tears meant for others are wept in front of the glass;
The confession is never posted; and the eye
Slides away from the proffered hand and discovers
An interesting view from the window.

The ridiculous mottled faces pass in stiff
Procession: relations, friends and chance encounters.
And the asinine minds that lie behind the gestures
Of goodness I can never reciprocate
Repel me with their inability
To escape from the grossest errors. Is it weakness
That sometimes imagines these shaped as heroes?
That cannot conceive of happiness as other
Than the apotheosis of the simple and kind?
That refuses to see how the century rises, pale,
From the death of its dream, ignoring the gains
Of the cruel, the different wishes of slaves?

The train removes me to another set
Of evasions. The valleys disappear. The train
Bolts through the central plain. I shall discover
Whether Lizzie Eustace retained her diamonds,
How far the hordes are from the city,
And my end will make significant for me
A casual place and date. My own child
Will grow from the generous warmth of his youth and perhaps
Discover, like me, that the solemn moments of life
Require their unbearable gaucheness translated to art.
For the guilt of being alive must be appeased
By the telling observation, and even feeling
Can only be borne retrospectively.
Bending over to kiss, the sensitive see with alarm
That their selves are still upright: the instant of death is announced
By a rattle of tin in the corridor. Meaning is given
These disparate happenings, our love is only
Revealed, by conventions: 'Dear Mother, I hope you are better.'
Or 'Lizzie resolved that she would have her revenge.'

The lilac will last a fortnight if the rain
Arrives, the sparrows will always turn to let
Their lime drop over the gutter, the gardener
Will lift the chickweed, and the clots of nests
In the elms disappear in the whirling green of summer.

At the end of the twilit road a figure is standing
Calling us to go in, while the far-off rumours
Of terrible facts which at last may destroy
Our happiness spoil our play. In the place we go to
The kettle boils on the fire, the brasses are polished,
But people are busy with pain in another room.
One night I shall watch the city and black sky meet
In the distance, the car lights stream on the heath like tracer,
And in such moments of lonely and mild exultation
This rhetoric will be forgotten, and the life of omission go on.
Behind me will lie the sad and convulsive events
As narrative art, and as fated, immortal and false.

TEN MEMORIAL POEMS
N.S. 1888—1949

Illness is to reconcile us to death

I

Week after week, month after month, in pain
You wrestled with that fiendish enemy –
The thing that tried in vain
To drag you from the room to its own territory.

Each day renewed the duel and our grief
Until at last upon the crumpled bed –
To our unwished relief –
The strange emaciated brown-faced fiend lay dead.

II

The image of the times that hurt me most
Were those blanched crawling creatures of the camps
Whose flesh was carved away
By fools and cruelty.

What horror that the object of our love
Should take that terrible symbolic shape
And guilt and fear release
From Europe to this house.

III

Your illness changed your life into a dream;
Its habits and its furniture became
The symbols of despair, our faces maps
Of odd utopias to which collapse
Had not as yet extended. In your head
Trembled the foreign language of the dead.

And yet you feigned an interest in our acts
As though the living were the permanent;
Like us, pretended to ignore the facts
That make the nightmare really what is meant.

Sometimes to please us you stretched for a cup
And smiled from that vile place where you lay bound:
Until you had to give our crude world up
And whisper what we couldn't understand.

IV

To think of your suffering and bear it,
The thought not the suffering:
That is the duty you gave me – unwittingly,
For you patiently took on the thing
To save me the sting.

To call forth a poem or so, it turns out,
Was your only appeal:
Perhaps you were conscious, fondly, that there too the gap
Between the idea and the real
Was too great to feel.

V

To understand the story
The innocent child assumes
A knowledge of jealousy
Or love. What ignorance looms,
What terrible feigning rages,
When death for us turns its pages!

Drug, legend, amulet,
Aphorism, prayer and tear,
To the truth approximate
Like scaffolding. The fear
Lives in the central lack
When the spars have been put back.

We can see dimly then
The hereditary fate
That comes to every man
In accidental shape,
Whose grotesque senselessness
Adds the sole sense to us.

VI

What irony that I can speak like this
Who rationed feeling when you were alive
To the half-felt but always studied kiss,
Dumb with the fear of those who run from love.

Now I can see, of course, our casual
But deep and strange relations from my birth,
How children must deny at every call
The embarrassing blood that links them to the earth.

My thoughts draw back like infinite generations.
Your parents do not know that you have died:
And now you have passed on to me the patience,
The loss, the care that one must try to hide.

Hoarding his gift for who must take it later,
The heir knows all the pangs of his testator.

VII

A year already since you died:
And I look back and see the vain
Lines I have written since the hour,
Frightened to turn to art that pain.

Art must create from human filth
And history's stupid lesson, hope.
Even in these atrocious days
Your death remains beyond my scope.

(136)

VIII

I imagine that simply to live is heroic,
Thinking of your death,
Forgetting the age will add to living
Its putrid breath.

IX

What first we feared for you we wished at last,
And death became a mentionable name,
As of an efficacious drug. So past
Ages preserved by love must in the shame

Of their decay call down an hourly curse.
And yet the age itself, in ignorance,
Desires to live; in its descent to worse
Heroic beyond the watcher's anxious stance.

O courage more than mine, you know a hope
That leaden evil days cannot offend:
For you death is unthinkable, its scope
Being no less than human suffering's end.

X

A long tense shadow falls across my page.
I flick the insect off the edge and know
What frightful light projects me on the age.

Between this south-east suburb and the glow
Of evening London turns a pitted face
Beneath a sky the colour of a blow.

Thinning and broadening as they check and race,
The ruins-loving birds that have returned
To haunt our cities take their resting place.

The horror of your pain and death that burned
Like acid in my chest now merges with
The duller but more constant gnawing learned

Through two long decades of a tragic myth.
The individual sorrow shrivels, leaving
Grief round the general sphere like bitter pith.

And in the larger body, also, heaving
Cells form irregular patterns that destroy
A hard-won alimentary achieving.

Yet since I found how pain supposes joy
I measure against man our weary Troy.

THE SNOW

The morning of the snow I walked alone
Through the deserted park, the bushes stone,
The snowless grass green shadows under yews,
Each footprint quick and violet as a bruise.

Empty of thought as was the sky of colour,
I saw the dead shoots blur the frozen pallor,
And turned into a narrow path between
The dirt of branches loaded with the clean.

What was it then that pierced my inmost self,
Walking alone along that little gulf:
What archetypal memory of cold,
What wolves, what forests, what unquiet child?

YOUTH REVISITED

The hastening cloud grows thin; the sun's pale disc
Swells, haloes, then bursts out and warms the stone,
Pitching the yew's black tent on brilliant green.
A dozen years have gone since last I saw
This tiny church set on the parkland's edge
Between the glistening hunters and the cattle,

A Sunday exercise for week-end guests,
And I approach it conscious that emotion
Ought to be suffered, as indeed it is.
Did I live here and was I happy then?
A war more innocent, an age of man
Removed, my poems thick with formal doom
And baseless faith in humans. Years that now
Pass with the clarity of hours then
Record the degeneration of the nerves
And the world situation, make a golden
Time from that decade of infirm belief.

I am half glad to find the place has marked
Dramatically my absence. All the roof
Has gone, grass flutters on the broken stone,
A notice says *These walls are dangerous.*
Through unglazed windows marble monuments
Are glimpsed like modest spinsters in their baths.
Bombs or neglect, informants are not sure:
In any case the church will now decay
With other luxuries. The horses are
Not here, no doubt the mansion house beyond
The lake is requisitioned by the state,
And furrows creep across the pleasure ground.

I wonder if my son completely fails
To grasp my halting reconstruction of
My youth. Here, where we brought you in our arms
Was neat then, facing time with fortitude.
The statues in the gloom stood for their moral,
The wicked viscount's smoke rose from the house,
The evils of the epoch had not quite
Made rational the artist's accidie.
And yet, the clock moved on another twelve,
You would have something still to put to your son.
The jet planes slither overhead, a frog
Throbs in the dust half-way across the road,
Over two fields a saw scrapes like a bird.
Creatures, machines and men live yet among
The partial, touching ruins of their world.

TIME

Stretched in the sun, I see upon my skin
A few and tiny violet veins, like worms –
Not shocked but as the sceptic viewer in
The lenses sees the plasm laced with germs.

The sun turns on, the body's pigmentation
Changes to flame: as gradually, the man
Accommodates the frightening situation,
The unlived years that fold up like a fan.

Time moves through matter at so queer a pace
One seldom sees it truly – sheer and vast.
Only in corners of the human space
Bruises reveal the struggle to hold fast:

Until time's final effort to be free
Involves the whole in stains and agony.

CÔTE DES MAURES

J.L.F., his poem

The azure marbled with white and palest grey:
The cactuses with buds like hand grenades:
The roman-candle palms: a lonely house
Against a hill, a wrong piece of a jig-saw.
The terraces descend in armour plating,
The grapes a violet shadow in their vines.
The gorgeous cobalt runs its washes up
Sienna bays. 'Colibris,' 'Les Flots Bleus,'
'Canadien's' – the memory retains
The *plages* like cheap tunes of a fatal year.

Two warships anchor in the gulf. The town
Suffers. A dog is begging by the sea,
Wearing a wrist watch, trousers, spectacles.

The images, instead of happiness,
Show once again the old compulsive shape:
The drama of unpurposed lives whose climax
Cannot evade the conventional pistol shot.
And the return to autumn: leaves that strew
Glass pavements under trees like ruined lace;
Reports from cruel, sentimental empires.

The traveller finds waters, brings his own
Disease. The poet's eye, impervious
To all except his fears, gives back a world
Dark, coloured, miniature, attractive, false.
The town that scabs the summit looks across
A land as densely folded as a pelt:
Below, the tide brings in its curious art.
Holding a knot of sea-turned wood, the bronze
Nude being sees through shores of culture bones
Of unadaptable enormities.

THE IMAGE

A spider in the bath. The image noted:
Significant maybe but surely cryptic.
A creature motionless and rather bloated,
The barriers shining, vertical and white:
Passing concern, and pity mixed with spite.

Next day with some surprise one finds it there.
It seems to have moved an inch or two, perhaps.
It starts to take on that familiar air
Of prisoners for whom time is erratic:
The filthy aunt forgotten in the attic.

Quite obviously it came up through the waste,
Rejects through ignorance or apathy
That passage back. The problem must be faced;
And life go on though strange intruders stir
Among its ordinary furniture.

One jibs at murder, so a sheet of paper
Is slipped beneath the accommodating legs.
The bathroom window shows for the escaper
The lighted lanterns of laburnum hung
In copper beeches – on which scene it's flung.

We certainly would like thus easily
To cast out of the house all suffering things.
But sadness and responsibility
For our own kind lives in the image noted:
A half-loved creature, motionless and bloated.

SENTIMENTAL POEM

In misty still October evenings
At the garden's end, attracted by the spade
Or mower, a bird comes on the fence and sings,
Prompted by whistling noises I have made.

Or so it seems – but one must guard against
The trap of the robin's sentimental name.
Maybe without me this soft throaty tensed
Recitative would go on just the same.

Because the bird half disappears upon
The dusky orange sunset sky, and will
Spring like a shade at solitary men
When others fly before the darkening wheel,

Do not imagine it can sympathise
Or love: no more than equal hope
These flowers with their yellow feline eyes
In lashes of unlikely heliotrope.

A brown leaf on a filament revolves.
Across the now-grey lawn the house lets fall
Its oblong lights: there human emblems move,
More plausible but no less strange and frail.

POEM TO PAY FOR A PEN

On the aeroplane from Nice I lost my pen,
That instrument of poetry and affairs.
Nor do I miss the coarser symbolism
The minor drama so naïvely bares.

In this the thirty-ninth year of my age,
Returned from those historic shores, it seems
That any old subject fits into my verse,
And there will stand for something else, like dreams.

The needle of the gramophone induces
The mood essential for the poet's art:
The sense of happiness, the huge ambition,
Last the few minutes to the record's heart.

The tides throw up the broken bits of culture
Perished when wine and oil gave way to coal:
The centre shifted to the provinces,
Drizzling and dull. The sun is to console.

And now the fecund centre shifts once more,
As all the life of capitals wears thin:
In gnawed rain-blackened buildings poets sit
Through wars of wanting neither side to win.

It shifts to where? Far from the world of pens,
And under suns too strong for wine or oil,
The tribes keep pure their healing savagery
And animal empires multiply and boil.

I do not know which are the most obscene:
Poets, profoundly sceptic, scared, unread:
The leaders monolithic in their mania;
Or the unteachable mass, as good as dead.

The solitary gramophone's entire
Repertoire is romantic; in the garden
The moonrise summons from its sullen fire
A yellow face that hurts but cannot pardon.

Moonlight, dark vegetation, ageing glands –
Those centuries-recurring aids to thought –
Bring up the never far away idea
Of humans shining virtuous as they ought.

This idealisation somehow is the real,
True like the fabulously moving strain
That with the grossest means, pen, gut and brass,
Resolves and then transcends the mortal pain.

THE TWO POETS

The one was witty and observant,
Words and translucent form his servant.
The other counted beats, weighed vowels,
His verse as thick and coiled as bowels.

The first died young. The second aged,
And, though officially he raged
Against the former, privately
Envied the light lost poetry.

Envied but never ceased to hope,
Thinking it still within his scope,
That unsought carelessness and truth
– The lucky manner of his youth.

TO A NOTEBOOK

You always open at unfinished pages.
Behind, the failures: daunting blanks ahead.
Here and not elsewhere my emotion rages.
Hungry for dreams you lie beside my bed.

An enemy to life, you give it hints
Of how to live: it still returns to you.
Yet your neglect means that my living stints
My life of all I feel, consider true.

You are the brilliant portrait that has made
Uneasy the nonentity it hired.
I'd like to end you but I am afraid,
Knowing that entry must be undesired.

Will you survive me? That's my constant care,
Living a miser for a doubtful heir.

PREFACE TO AN ANTHOLOGY

Don't be deceived, some poems printed here
May merely illustrate the condemnation
Of the anthologist: omission were
Too vague a sign to show his detestation.

Nor has he chosen of the verse he likes
That he thinks quite the best: he aimed to prove
A theory in this volume, as one looks
On an old wife with warm complacent love.

With quiet pride he added just too few
Examples of his own successful work:
If the thing as a whole should fail he knew
There was at least one signpost in the murk.

Anthologists not always have the wit
To see it is their passion that abets
The gradual ruin of their choice: that what
Their pages fail to stale history forgets.

ON READING A SOVIET NOVEL

Will not the Local Party Secretary
Prove that his love of men's not innocent:
The heroine at last be blown off course
By some base, gusty, female element:
And the grave hero be eventually torn
By a disgraceful infantile event?

No, in this world the good works out its course
Unhindered by the real, irrelevant flaw.
Our guilty eyes glaze over with ennui
At so much honest purpose, rigid law.
This is not life, we say, who ask that art
Show mainly what the partial butler saw.

And yet with what disquiet we leave the tale!
The mere appearance of the descending Goth,
So frightful to a sedentary race,
Made him invincible. It is not wrath
That breaks up cultures but the virtues of
The stupid elephant, the piddling moth.

The threatened empire dreads its rival's arms
Less than the qualities at which it sneers –
The slave morality promoted to
A way of life: naïve, old-fashioned tears
Which once it shed itself by bucketsful
In nascent, optimistic, long-dead years.

TWO POEMS FROM BAUDELAIRE

CATS

Lovers and austere dons are equally
(In their maturity) attached to cats –
Cats soft but cruel, emperors of flats,
Touchy like these and like those sedentary.

Friends of the sensual, the cerebral,
They seek the quiet and horror of the dark;
If they had ever bent their pride to work
They might have pulled the funeral cars of hell.

Asleep they take the noble attitude
Of the great sphinxes that appear to brood,
Stretched in the wastes, in dreams that have no end;

Their loins are electric with fecundity,
And particles of gold, like finest sand,
Star vaguely their unfathomable eye.

OWLS

Swaddled in yews as black as ink
The owls sit in a tidy frieze
Like oriental deities,
Unlidding their red eyes. They think.

They will sit on quite motionless
Until that hour, nostalgic, dun,
When, rolling up the slanting sun,
Shadows reoccupy the place.

Their attitude reminds the clever
That in our time and world one never
Ought to seek action, or revolt;

Man shaken by a creeping shade
Bears always in himself the guilt
Of having wished to change his fate.

ANDRÉ GIDE

After a night of insomnia I read
In the morning paper of the death of Gide,
Who by allowing smaller men to share
Such nights of his made theirs the less to bear,
Even to answer to creative need.

Himself an instrument through which events
Become translated into measurements,
His death makes, like a father's ending or
The long-anticipated start of war,
An alteration in the epoch's tense.

Whatever routes the intellectuals haunt
Around the actions of their times will want
The practical travel notes of Gide; and feel
The spirit of the illusory and real
– That figure, thin-lipped, passionate and gaunt.

A general hope hung on him with the weight
Of intimate anxieties; and yet
He carefully made plain the consolations
Of an earth colonised, he knew, by nations
Pregnant not with amelioration – hate.

All contradictions were resolved in art:
Utopias in bad taste, the gulfs that part
The individual life from what it sees
As fated but grotesque realities,
Writer from age which yet must feed his heart.

Now he becomes the earth he praised, in spite
Of art: but as when in the desperate night,
Sleepless, we switch the lamp out finally,
To our unwished and sad relief we see
Behind the curtain leap another light.

IBSEN

Some of the symbols are ridiculous.
The drain, the tower – these do not even mean
What one expects them to.
They clump across the stage
As obvious as wigs.

A minute later one is not so sure.
The drain transmits blood laced with spirochetes.
The tower is not ideals
Nor sex but one of those
Emblems without a key:

And all the high stiff collars and the ledgers
Shine out with their own intense interior meaning:
    The names like fiords, the
    Chorus of doctors, take
    Their place in consummate verse.

Ibsen revealed that the symbol had a past,
That crude interpretation could be stripped
    Of rings of time, to find
    Inside the foliate five
    Acts the small pulsing germ.

ON SPALDING'S *HANDBOOK TO PROUST*

Like life the novel's just too long to grasp:
Perhaps an index will show what they mean.
Over a hundred entries deal with LOVE –
Alas! – almost two hundred ALBERTINE.

The index drives us back into the text,
The text to life; until we see again
How they both hover on the edge of what
The entries of an index would explain.

NECROPHAGY

The jelly baby is a kind of sweet,
    It actually has eyes;
And held up to the light its little corpse
    Bears the transparencies
    And flaws of realer size.

These soft smooth bodies lie in heaps, and if
    One is picked up the rest
Tend to cling to it in mixed attitudes,
    So first you must divest
    The victim of the nest.

(149)

Some eat the jelly baby whole but most
　　Dismember it at leisure,
For, headless, there is no doubt that it gives
　　A reasonable measure
　　Of unexampled pleasure.

About the jelly baby other things
　　Occur to me: the fact
That eating it brings back the feelings of
　　Our infancy; the act
　　Of choosing black with tact;

And finally that in its rigid arms
　　Held close against its side,
And absolute identity with others,
　　Its pathos and fate reside,
　　That else it had not died.

TRANSLATION

Now that the barbarians have got as far as Picra,
And all the new music is written in the twelve-tone scale,
And I am anyway approaching my fortieth birthday,
　　I will dissemble no longer.

I will stop expressing my belief in the rosy
Future of man, and accept the evidence
Of a couple of wretched wars and innumerable
　　Abortive revolutions.

I will cease to blame the stupidity of the slaves
Upon their masters and nurture, and will say,
Plainly, that they are enemies to culture,
　　Advancement and cleanliness.

From progressive organisations, from quarterlies
Devoted to daring verse, from membership of
Committees, from letters of various protest
　　I shall withdraw forthwith.

When they call me reactionary I shall smile,
Secure in another dimension. When they say
'Cinna has ceased to matter' I shall know
    How well I reflect the times.

The ruling class will think I am on their side
And make friendly overtures, but I shall retire
To the side further from Picra and write some poems
    About the doom of the whole boiling.

Anyone happy in this age and place
Is daft or corrupt. Better to abdicate
From a material and spiritual terrain
    Fit only for barbarians.

INACTION

Writers entrapped by teatime fame and by commuters' comforts –
MARIANNE MOORE

A strange dog trots into the drive, sniffs, turns
And pees against a mudguard of my car.
I see this through the window, past *The Times*,
And drop my toast and impotently glare.

But indignation gives way to unease.
Clearly the dog, not merely impudent,
Was critical of man's activities,
Mine in particular, I'm forced to grant.

And so the entertainment of the morning
Headlines is temporarily spoiled for me:
During my coffee I must heed their warning,
The fate of millions take half seriously.

Inadequate, I know, this old concern,
Only productive of a quickened pulse,
A hanging jacket that gives one a turn.
The sneering dog demanded something else.

SOCIALIST'S SONG

It was an ex-sailor grown old in the war
Who'd learnt many swear words and how to tie knots;
A month in a barracks and then a month more,
A convoy between and some curious spots.
    Tattooed in Bombay
    Always short in his pay,
His wife never out of the family way.
Not early on duty but not really late;
Five fags and a parrot were all his estate.
Oh this is the man who must suffer the fate
Of being the only support of the state.

Demobbed with a mac and a smell of the truth,
A promise of peace and a couple of gongs,
And all that remained of six years of his youth,
Some dirty and some sentimental old songs.
    Then back to the shop,
    The two-shilling hop,
And all the same faces still there at the top.
Still paid for the job at just under the rate,
A pint and a council house all his estate.
Oh this is the man who must suffer the fate
Of being the only support of the state.

Now what do you think, he is wanted again,
This teased-out old stripey with cracks in his neck;
He's wanted again for his muscle and brain –
The Oerlikon gun and an acre of deck.
    It may be the West
    That will lay him to rest
Or Asia provide him a watery vest;
Wherever he is on that terrible date
A fathom of canvas will be his estate.
For this is the man who must suffer the fate
Of being the only support of the state.

Can anything happen to add to the pleasure
Of life and improve the sad tone of this song?

Allow the ex-sailor to die at his leisure,
Decrease the superfluous measure of wrong?
      Yes, country and town
      Could turn upside down,
Dislodging director, policeman and crown,
And fall in the lap of this man without hate –
Two hands and a family all his estate –
And truly permit him to suffer the fate
Of being the only support of the state.

A WET SUNDAY IN SPRING

Symptoms at high altitudes:
Emaciation and overstrain.
Life at high latitudes: small wingless flies
Capable of living for long periods
In a frozen state.

I sit in the inventive temperate zone,
Raised only by the city's floors of culture,
Watching the rain bombard the lilac, feeling
The radio come in round me like a tide.
Deafness let Beethoven escape the tyranny
Of concord: some such mutation should exclude this age
From having to admit the possibility
Of happiness.
            The ivory-horned chestnut
Effortlessly assumes its tasks; the rain
Is perpendicular and horribly fertile;
The embattled green proliferates like cells.
I think feebly of man's wrong organisations,
Incurable leaders, nature lying in wait
For weakness like an animal or germ,
And aircraft growling in the summer air.

TIMES OF WAR AND REVOLUTION

The years reveal successively the true
Significance of all the casual shapes
Shown by the atlas. What we scarcely knew
Becomes an image haunting as a face;
Each picture rising from neglected place
To form the dial of our cursor hopes,
As that undreamt-of frontier slowly writhes
Along the wishes of explosive, lives.

The pages char and turn. Our memories
Fail. What emotions shook us in our youth
Are unimaginable as the truth
Our middle years pursue. And only pain
Of some disquieting vague variety gnaws,
Seeing a boy trace out a map of Spain.

WINTER ROUNDEL

From shapes like men fog thickens in the street
And London grows as lonely as a fen:
A muffled shout, a dangerous sound of feet,
    From shapes like men.

The solstice nears, the armistice again
Recedes; the pavements of our world retreat,
And lovers huddle closer in their den.

The deadly particles of matter greet,
Less hypothetical, the physicists' ken:
Paralysed cities wait a solar heat
    From shapes like men.

THE FIFTIES

The wretched summers start again
With lies and armies ready for
Advancing on that fast terrain.

Like those of China, Poland, Spain,
With twenty territories more,
The wretched summers start again.

The rumours and betrayals stain
The helpless millions of the poor
Advancing on that fast terrain.

Asian and European rain
Falls from between the blue of yore:
The wretched summers start again.

And rubble and the jungle gain
A foothold on the cultured shore,
Advancing on that fast terrain.

Short youth was shortened by the pain
Of seasons suitable for war:
The wretched summers start again,
Advancing on that fast terrain.

THE MEETING

At the ineffective meeting is received
　　The letter: 'From your guilt
I resign. I exculpate myself from all
　　Your pistols and libels.

'I shall devote myself henceforth to God
　　And the investigation of freedom.
I write from a country cottage where the chestnut
　　Makes miniature

'Images of itself with its sea-scum blossom.
　　Your world is urban and evil.
My cat advises me: remove my name, please,
　　From your list of dog-lovers.'

The committee composes its reply: 'We, too,
   Have seen that tree in spring
Making pink blotting paper of the lawns.
    And as for the shootings

'They were of those who would have let art die
   With lovely anaemia.
Your cat is right: his name has been embossed
    On our notepaper.

'Consider: we need your support who are able even
   To formulate the questions.
Try to recover the original impulse
    That led you to join us.

'For the season now is nearly over and
   The orators put away
Their stools. The belting slows. The tubes are about
    To leap from their racks.'

PANTOMIME

Steeped in a mouldy light, the frightful Witch
Proclaims excessively the power of evil.
Surely there is no need to emphasise
The eventual triumph of the cyst and weevil.

And yet the Fairy seems quite confident,
Promising that good will eventually reign
In the divided kingdom, rising superior
To tattered tinsel and blue pathetic vein.

True enough, the foolish but kindly Prince is restored,
The lovers promise to live happily ever after,
The chorus of agricultural labourers
Is heard in apparently genuine laughter.

Is there no epilogue of realism?
Do the trapdoors which led to lower regions
Remain fast shut upon the destructive thoughts
And heavily armoured and most fatal legions?

DEATH OF A DICTATOR

The children years ago made their escape
Out of the father's tense, oppressive field:
His moral scheme was of too strict a shape
To hold the freedom that their growth revealed.

Now he lies bound and senseless up the stair,
Drowned by the failing channels of his flesh,
They momentarily return and wear
The old familiar pressure of the mesh.

They wait among the ugly furniture,
Rich with the poignant memories of their youth:
Once more they feel that agonising blur –
The hopeless falsehood merging into truth.

And still perceive a sprig of what their hate
Grew up with and then choked – but all too late.

NINO, THE WONDER DOG

A dog emerges from the flies
    Balanced upon a ball.
Our entertainment is the fear
    Or hope the dog will fall.

It comes and goes on larger spheres,
    And then walks on and halts
In the centre of the stage and turns
    Two or three somersaults.

The curtains descend upon the act.
    After a proper pause
The dog comes out between them to
    Receive its last applause.

Most mouths are set in pitying smiles,
    Few eyes are free from rheum:
The sensitive are filled with thoughts
    Of death and love and doom.

No doubt behind this ugly dog,
   Frail, fairly small, and white,
Stands some beneficent protector,
   Some life outside the night.

But this is not apparent as
   It goes, in the glare alone,
Through what it must to serve absurd-
   ities beyond its own.

IMAGES OF AUTUMN

In pools made by the brown and golden litter
That chokes the grids, stand tinted grey reflections
Of branches with their few leaves hung
Against a cloudy sky. The autumn flood
Of symbols pile behind the poet's sluices.

But his new interest in the world is not
Reciprocated, and it ploughs on toughly
Through rhododendron scrub infested with
Leeches, the pre-deflation plunge in Kaffirs,
And tests of tinier bombs to atomise

Troops in the field. The poet pays for this
Indifference, or rather for his themes'
Irrelevance – those same Tormentors which
Started on Cowper and which really are
Such thoughts as a clerkship in the House of Lords.

Leaves stream from dying trees like yellow birds,
And the nations' situation degenerates.
Like eaters of sweets, they are sick but cannot stop;
Like lovers, perversely go on saying things
That hurt. The poet wishes to be noticed

But only gets a pat: he can recite
Tomorrow, but just now must go to bed.
He notes that wheels have stamped on the macadam
The sodden leaves like a design on stuff:
And the image opens seldom-opened doors.

If this were all, if this solution answered
More than the egotistic wish for art,
For fame as death's opponent, and laid bare
That shattering historical event
Unknown to both the analyst and patient,

There would be no need to imagine mornings
Whose social truths would correspond to those
When after nights of storm one finds, outside,
The sky unusually pale and empty,
And in the gutters thick and rustling treasure.

POET AND READER

Your verses are depressing,
Obsessed with years and death:
Don't you observe the blessing
In merely drawing breath,
In things that aren't so pressing?

Remember, please, my verse
Comes out of moods of pleasure,
If life were any worse
There wouldn't be the leisure
Even to moan and curse.

The very act of warning
Implies a faith in readers:
It's not quite you I'm mourning,
Rather the seedy leaders
You are for ever spawning.

All art foresees a future,
Save art which fails to weigh
The sadness of the creature,
The limit of its day,
Its losing war with nature.

VI

IV

SPRING SONG

Behind the plate glass of hotels
Old ladies watch the savage sea;
The adolescent casts his spells
On ignorant reality;
And every girl is made by time
Tragic beyond her silly power;
And still the poet in his rhyme
'Accept, accept', cries from his tower.

Upon a gate in carven stone
Two armoured torsos sneer with pride;
The empires riddled to the bone
As sick men stand, who stand and hide
A mortal sickness; and the poet,
Like the great apes, in childhood gay
Morose thereafter dare not show it:
'Accept, accept', his verses say.

Irises point indecent buds
Beside the withered daffodils;
Tender lascivious feeling floods
The veins that show, the heart that kills;
And where the wry-mouthed fledgling crawls
With busy termite citizens
The sentimental poet bawls
'Accept, accept', through blinding lens.

The 'cellist from between his knees
Sends out a transcendental chord;
Suddenly cherry branches freeze;
The captain points across the ford;
Conception lags behind the world
That dreams and poetry reveal:
The grub within its shining curled
'Accept, accept', is heard to squeal.

SUMMER

From estuary to channel
White explosions of cloud;
The charming cyclists tunnel
Through the leaf-shadowed road.
Fate's motto theme suspended
Under long arpeggios
Of warmth and light; unhanded
Unjustly-sentenced youth.
Each bill and torrent cries
An indubitable truth.

All living matter's power
To reproduce its form
Includes occasional error:
In air and water swarm,
Gorgeous beyond their title,
The creatures; and the mother
Sends out into the battle
Past her retreating force
Fresh notions of brow and feather
To perpetuate the race.

Desire could gaze for ever
Where in the dark meniscus
Sparkles the imaged river.
O lovers, fabulous maskers,
Enjoy your day: too soon
Swans whitening the dusk
Above the magician's fane
Will announce the long dominion
Of loss. What shall you ask?
To see in your companion,

If only for a curt
Moment, potentials as moving
As the materials of art.
The universe of loving
Is not this summer, even,

Where far into the night
Blossom and owl make known
Perfume and grove, but wrong
Cells that the strange create
From which the conquerors spring.

PICTURES OF WINTER

Whips, river systems, hands of mandarins –
With trees on skies the inventive mood begins.

After the gallery's rich, vivid hoard
The still, grey river stabs me with its sword.

Behind the city the unmoving west
Burns smoky-orange like a robin's breast.

At four o'clock the living-room window frames
A faded photograph of roofs and flames.

Stepping outside the muffled house I freeze
Beneath calm, radiant immensities.

In the cold air the breath clouds of a horse
Fade, whiten, fed by two cones from their source.

Under my feet the snow cries out like mice,
Its feathers left behind compressed to ice.

Night, and the snow descending on the high
Branches now scarcely darker than the sky.

Décor of wolves and puppets, swans and dreams –
A snow-hung garden in a street-lamp's beams.

Closing the curtains, through the yellow light
I see a whiteness where it should be night.

The tangerine belies its glowing form,
But shivering bodies find each other warm.

Strange this new colour of the world I know;
Strange as my ginger cat upon the snow.

A general weeping from boughs still severe
Moves the heart with the turning hemisphere.

The puffed white blossom in the garden urn
Dissolves to earth that holds a queen's return.

I dig the soil and in its barren cold
Surprise a bulb-bomb fused with palest gold.

But still the knouts and veins divide the air,
Save for their swelling buds of sparrows, bare.

AUTOBIOGRAPHY OF A LUNGWORM

My normal dwelling is the lungs of swine,
    My normal shape a worm,
But other dwellings, other shapes, are mine
    Within my natural term.
Dimly I see my life, of all, the sign,
    Of better lives the germ.

The pig, though I am inoffensive, coughs,
    Finding me irritant:
My eggs go with the contents of the troughs
    From mouth to excrement –
The pig thus thinks, perhaps, he forever doffs
    His niggling resident.

The eggs lie unconsidered in the dung
    Upon the farmyard floor,
Far from the scarlet and sustaining lung:
    But happily a poor
And humble denizen provides a rung
    To make ascension sure.

The earthworm eats the eggs; inside the warm
    Cylinder larvae hatch:
For years, if necessary, in this form
    I wait the lucky match
That will return me to my cherished norm,
    My ugly pelt dispatch.

Strangely, it is the pig himself becomes
    The god inside the car:
His greed devours the earthworms; so the slums
    Of his intestines are
The setting for the act when clay succumbs
    And force steers for its star.

The larvae burrow through the bowel wall
    And, having to the dregs
Drained ignominy, gain the lung's great hall.
    They change. Once more, like pegs,
Lungworms are anchored to the rise and fall
    – And start to lay their eggs.

What does this mean? The individual,
    Nature, mutation, strife?
I feel, though I am simple, still the whole
    Is complex; and that life –
A huge, doomed throbbing – has a wiry soul
    That must escape the knife.

ON GRAZING A FINGER

In time and place such wounds are staggered;
Healing, too, holds them in dominion.
I am most thankful: under the surface
A ghastly thing moves on its skeleton.

ELEMENTARY PHILOSOPHY

White blossom in the room:
And, stepping in the gloom
The pallid garden wears,
I watch the glowing disc
Indigo cloud unbares
And feel the human risk.

Four thousand million years
Have hatched these staggering fears,
And years that lie ahead
Of equal amplitude,
With man alive or dead,
Can never heal the feud.

Planets and stars alone
To destinies unknown,
This universe and more
For monstrous, alien reasons,
Journey beyond our four
Senses and local seasons.

I go back to the flowers,
The house's love and hours,
But still I see this spring,
That buds with final wars,
Foam from some heaving thing
Blown over endless shores.

THE DAY

At the time it seemed unimportant: he was lying
In bed, off work, with a sudden pain,
And she was haloed by the morning sun,
Enquiring if he'd like the daily paper.

So idle Byzantium scarcely felt at first
The presence in her remoter provinces
Of the destructive followers of the Crescent.

But in retrospect that day of moderate health
Stood fired in solid and delightful hues,
The last of joy, the first of something else –
An inconceivable time when sex could be
Grasped for the asking with gigantic limbs,
When interest still was keen in the disasters
Of others – accident, uprising, drouth –
And the sharp mind perceived the poignancy
Of the ridiculous thoughts of dissolution.

A day remembered by a shrivelled empire
Nursed by hermaphrodites and unsustained
By tepid fluids poured in its crying mouth.

ON A TEXTBOOK OF SURGERY

Dear fellow-humans, what
Inhuman deformities
And highly-coloured growths
Your colourless flesh can suffer!

Keepers of fish in ponds
Sometimes clip off with scissors
The fungus that exudes
From those dumb swimming creatures.

I would not, myself, keep fish.
Or, if compelled, would at
The term of their bright youth
Kill or not visit them.

TO A GIRL IN THE MORNING

Hair blurred by slumber still;
The dreams in which you moved
Towards such prodigies
As loving and being loved
Slow gently, like a hill,

Your limbs; and in your eyes
I see myself transformed
To what Circe once charmed.

Before your innocence
And infinite desire,
Wisdom and age will stagger
And start to doubt their power,
While you recite the tense
That drives a yearning dagger
In those who know what scar
Future and past must score.

The thought that generations
Spring to infinity,
Could formerly sustain
Such death-racked men as I,
But now the state of nations
Threatens a burnt-out strain,
And you may be the last
Of those who have moved my lust.

ECLIPSE

January 19, 1954: 12.50–4.13

So last night while we slept the moon
Crawled through the shadow's long black spear,
Finding in all that sun-ruled void
The darkness of the human sphere.

Our dreams were as incredible.
The little bodies froze, and then
Their longings soared and fell on worlds
Too distant for the years of men.

Tonight across the unflawed moon
Clouds like the ribbing of a shore
Pass endlessly, and life and planet
Take their far stations as before.

I pass into the house which wears,
As architecture must, its age:
Upon the rotting floor the moon
Opens its pure utopian page.

DISCREPANCIES

Even smooth, feared executives have leisure
To show the inadequacy of their love:
    The longest day must end
    In animal nakedness.

And in the city what amused our fathers –
Sledgehammers wielded by dwarfs to mark the hours –
    Move us as emblems of
    Something quite terrible.

Gazing upon us as we cross the courtyard
Of the exchange, on our legitimate business,
    Are frenzied masks of stone
    With clutching human hands.

And we imagine what unthinkable shape
A girl's slim velvet shoe conceals that strolls
    The pavements of boulevards
    Carrying intestines of sewers.

A man at the floor of his destination finds –
Inexplicably for a moment – the same defect,
    As at the start of his journey,
    In the lift's inner gate.

And the emperor, drenched in scents from realms too far
To visit, cannot know that history
    Will not record the name
    Of his son teasing the peacocks.

But eras when the sensitive reported
Doom through the deformation of a pot,
    False quantities, and sounds
    Too harsh for memory,

Were secretly incubating even then
Bravery out of freaks, ethics from hate
    And valid economies
    Of starving theorists.

In trying to be just our systems hunt:
Too violent man's feed-back. Hector's shield
    Lies under a massive floor
    Of hideous ornaments.

The sublimations of the poets rise
From their renunciation of coarse hair
    And the inanities
    Of ravishing crimson lips.

NIGHT PIECE

    Through the gentle poet's sleep
    Visages of marble weep,
    While around their smutted plinths
    Virgins, books and hyacinths
    Are undone by fetid beasts.
    What sagacious leeches, priests,
    Can absterge the petalled floor
    Or unbar the censor's door
    To fresh vistas where those lusts
    Rank behind the gnostic busts,
    And the violations seem
    Made from that excessive dream
    Which a painter has when he
    Finishes reality
    And beyond the wrinkled brows,
    Through slim pilasters or boughs,
    Paints upon the flowery hill
    Little men that run and kill?
    None: the contradictions of
    Prone Lucrece and selfless love
    Rise from that abstruse machine
    Which the gross cells did not mean

With their purely sensual making.
In the rationale of waking
Only edges of the harm
Can protrude into our calm:
For example, that still sphere,
Bloody, quartered, very near,
In a portion of the sky
Fateful to man's destiny;
Or that through long vapour rides
Coldly drawing lethal tides;
Or that simply glows among
Worlds indifferent to wrong,
Mocking even that remote
Name of huntress that she got
From the temples now that lie
Broken in her violet eye.
When this race that can support
Weak, creative men who court
Constantly the very dread
In the imaginative head
Which the race by conquering
Overcame the previous thing –
When this race has vanished, who
Will observe the silvered yew
Springing out of pits of dark
In the breathings of the park,
Or the calculable rise
Of the strangely blazing skies
Signalling a prince's woe?
All will then exist as though
Purposelessness were its end;
Orbits of the planets bend
Silent on their parallels,
With their living carbon shells
In such rich fantastic shapes
As gigantic ferns and apes –
Dying, judged by clocks that freeze
Filled with cogs of galaxies.
As it would exist in fact
Did we not before the act

Place the necessary lens:
Howling satellites and dense
Gas-swathed orbs towards us glide
As a harmless lantern slide;
And the native human hope,
That reversing telescope,
Makes extinction seem so small
As not to be there at all.
Readings given by the blunt
Instrument, our body, shunt
Merely symbols from a truth
That exists cocksure, uncouth,
Sprawling over species, ages,
Universes; and whose rages
Made the flying algebra
Of this night of moon and star.

AMBIGUITIES

A blackbird, rather worn about the eyes,
Flaps down beside me as I clip the grass.
From its clenched bill protrudes a withered mass
Which with a sickened pity I surmise
To be the fronds of some malignancy
That drives the bird to human company.

But it contrives to take a garish moon
Of caterpillar in that beak, and flies
Away before the ambiguities
Of pain and greed can be resolved. Too soon
The questions are withdrawn that can demand
Answers we dare not give or understand.

The age regards me from the summer sky
Where aircraft slowly chalk the blue with frost,
And from these crumpled, hopeless headlines tossed
Upon the ageless fire. And while I try
To balance barren anger and despair
The creamy smoke boils upright in the air,

And drifts away above the trees and streets,
And mingles with the haze from factories –
Organs that raised us, now monstrosities –
That lie along the river bank like fleets.
The moving power of verse, as Hopkins said,
Is love, and that emotion, if not dead,

For me is thwarted by the manifest
Falsehood of holy books that forecast good.
The dying must be loathed, although we would
Look on them differently; and the confessed
And chronic choice by history of error
Prints on the normal face a mask of terror.

The ignorance and daftness of the mass:
Are they irrelevant? I only know
That pity is the best that I can show,
Conscious that pity merely blurs the glass
Which should send back an image, flawed maybe,
But past such little human tragedy.

EXPOSTULATION AND INADEQUATE REPLY

I wish you would write a poem, in blank verse,
addressed to those who, in consequence of the
complete failure of the French Revolution,
have thrown up all hopes of the amelioration
of mankind, and are sinking into an almost
epicurean selfishness, disguising the same
under the soft titles of domestic attachment
and contempt for visionary philosophes. –
Coleridge to Wordsworth, 1799.

Alas! dear Coleridge, I am not the man,
After a century and a half, to write
That poem – of another Revolution
And yet another generation of

Poets who, since the age holds out no hope,
Abjure the age and its attempted changers,
Trying to find in personal love their tropes
For poetry and reason for their lives.
It will not do: their verse is sloppy and
Their beings trivial or meaningless.
For still the active world maintains the turn
It took when you were young, and posed against
Its harsh demands for truth and sacrifice
The useless poet must arrange himself
With care if he is not to be an adjunct
Reactionary or irrelevant.
Of course, my only difference is I know
How weak I am, what strength the times require:
Attempting to disown the spurious virtue
That springs from guilt and from the making out
Of paths I dare not tread.

                                    I wonder how
(Writing these lines beneath the gentle gold
That streams obliquely from the branches soon
To show entirely their essential structure)
Precisely you regarded that autumnal
World which arrived so quickly after spring.
Could you imagine yet another chance
For tyranny to die, for men to make
An order of equality and right?
You did not sink, I know, immediately
Into acceptance of the status quo,
The old lies and the old injustices.
And history, although you could not tell,
Was gathering up the scattered elements
To make in time another grand assault
Upon the barricades of privilege,
Islands of class, the beaches of selfish atoms,
And will again, though it's our tragedy
– And opportunity – that history
Is only the totality of action
By many men who each alone are blind
To what they do, and may do.

Seen far off
The forest's million bones are smudged with bands
Of bistre, raw sienna, faded green.
Sad season of the end of growth, the start
Of cold that seems, in this faint sun, will be
Unbearable! And yet it will be borne,
And those who can survive will find the new,
Delicate but sure republic of the crocus,
The warm fraternal winds, the growing strength
Of wheat and apple's equal luxury.
This could not be the poem you desired.
We grow to understand that words alone,
The visionary gleam through which the poet
More and more consciously, less frequently,
Renews his youth, are, like all art, condemned
To failure in the sense that they succeed.
You, who so early lost that power, know best
How men forever seek, not quite in vain,
Sublime societies of imagination
In worlds like this, and that no more exist.

A SONG BETWEEN TWO SHEPHERDS

1. *Shep.*   Upon this pasture scarred and brown
         I find it hard to feed my flocks:
         What's left by the invading town
         Between the factory and the rocks
             Has been the battered shore
             Of swinging tides of war.

2. *Shep.*   Why trouble to sustain the breed
         Since soon the heat and aims of hell
         Released from that exploding seed
         Will change the pattern in the cell:
             Rich chops, wool thick and frore,
             Be born to you no more?

1. *Shep.*   Though shepherds always will complain
         Of shepherdesses and of grass,
         Hoping for love without its pain,

(177)

Fat sheep from hills of hidden brass,
                 Only they will ensure
                 Survival of the poor.

2. *Shep.*   The inorganic shapes that prank,
             Fortuitously, monstrously,
             Our mineral star's indifferent flank
             Already count their tenancy
                 In years of famine or
                 The first armed hours of war.

1. *Shep.*   My sheep are no more strange than this
             Blue planet that now winks above
             The dusky wood; my shepherdess
             No briefer than the craving love
                 For magnet of the ore,
                 Of orbit for the core.

2. *Shep.*   Shepherd, I see in you the dupe
             Of happiness, the weakling who
             Finds warmth in huddling with the group,
             And wishes what he felt were true.
                 This lank flock, withered ear,
                 Accept for what they are.

1. *Shep.*   Shepherd, I must survey with sorrow
             My pasture trenched with arms and street,
             Yet I will hope to see a morrow
             When sheep and town will join to meet
                 Real enemies – the four
                 Seasons, man's last half score.

PLEASURE DRIVE

Children play on the by-pass, with the peaks
Of gasometers haunting them, and factories
Like lingering shapes of the past. Beyond, in fields,
Are massive artificial animals
And haystacks like Tibetan hats – the strange

(178)

Art of the simple. Lanes lead to villages
Selling beer and petrol as stores to mad explorers:
Behind the walls are superstitious rites,
Performed under pious mottoes worked in wool.

And so to higher land whose fortifications
Date back to fathers with somewhat smaller brains.
The roads and churches in the valley sink
Beneath old vegetation: further still
The opposing line of downs is menacing
As a rival system.

                   Now we descend, the wind
Fresher, tinctured with chemicals, through
Light industries, across the estuary's bridge.
The point of this provincial city is
A tower that kept the river from the sea,
Particular from general. Like a rotten tooth,
Its walls disguise an empty centre where
Hundreds of birds festoon the greyish air,
Their droppings falling through the rooms of state
To pile up in the dungeons. In the squares
Of battlements fit sections of the city:
The railway's claws, the suburbs spread like fans,
And in a moat of green the similar
Cathedral stone, a different kind of ruin.

Time has irregularities, its grain
Leaves knots where the unfortunate remain,
Hacking against irrational designs.
Let us return to that metropolis
Whose fuming lights the sky, whose galleries
Blaze with ingenious art, whose sewers flow,
Where those in love are glad and soldiers only
Polish euphoniums and horses' rumps;
And not despise its anachronistic pleasures.
Even when classes do not slay each other
And generations accept their heritage,

(179)

In times of monolithic calm, the single
Life must enjoy its happiness between
Atrocious thoughts: the smiling driver who
Forever nears that unwished destination
Where his road ends in blood and wrecked machine.

WINTER WORLD

A clouded sky at dusk the dirty red
Of grazed skin: slightly furred, the trees, as though
Drawn with a fine pen on a still-damp wash:
               The river slow.

Over the black and echoing viaduct
Golden-barred trains stretch out and glide like snakes.
The swans precede converging, crimson and grey
               Dissolving wakes.

Some by the lapping brink assume the long
Contorted shapes of heraldry or dreams,
And one swells to that myth where girl with god
               Equally gleams.

Their beaks are rough and chill: I let the bread
Fall to the gravel which contains the bones
Of birds and men, coins of dead dynasties,
               And ice age stones.

The poem should end here, its *trouvailles* all
Exhausted, but there still remains the moral –
The aggregate of all the lives in time,
               That reef of coral.

The lyricist in a technician's age, the castle
In the cathedral's, and the single life
Born in an era of universal doom,
               Still, like a wife,

Look to an eventually happy time, in the teeth
Of the evidence. And during Rome's most dread
Decline the barbarians were enjoying themselves,
                    As Whitehead said.

The Faustian image: I am one of those
Whose skull will be discovered; but its whole
Consciousness then sucked out, long since surrendered
                    Its gloomy soul.

Tonight the swans, tomorrow the marble leader
Disfigured with tears of droppings – everywhere
Poets of the final period find themes
                    For their despair:

Always they see their bodies, not their work,
Consorting with that vanished world which must
Present itself noble in pathos, inevitable, to
                    The sifters of its dust.

FLORESTAN TO LEONORA

Our shadows fall beyond the empty cage.
The Minister has gone and I am left
To try to live with your heroic age.

I spare a thought, my dear, for you who must
Go home to change the jackboots for a skirt
And put the pistol on its nail to rust;

But mainly think of my impossible task.
My own love might have tried what yours achieved:
It cannot bear the gift it did not ask.

After the trumpet I felt, in our embrace,
I had been cheated of the captured's right
To innocent inaction and to face

A suffering unjust as a sarcoma.
Did you never conceive that it was possible
To like incarceration? In this trauma

Of the imprisoning era there must be
Some prisoners – for torturers to visit,
To wear the pallor and the beards of free

Philosophers, and tap on streaming walls
Their selfless ineffective messages
Concerning liberty to brutish cells.

When the mob sang of brotherhood and joy
I was embarrassed, more so when I saw
The near-erotic answer in your eye.

You take my hand as though I ought to live;
And lead me out to that alarming world
Which, the oppressor dead, the sensitive

Can find inimical no longer. Yes,
Our values must shrivel to the size of those
Held by a class content with happiness;

And warmed by our children, full of bread and wine,
I shall dream of the discipline of insomnia
And an art of symbols, starved and saturnine.

THE IDES OF MARCH

Fireballs and thunder augment the wailing wind:
A vulgar score, but not inappropriate
To my romantic, classic situation.
Within the house my wife is asleep and dreaming
That I, too, am cocooned inside the world
Of love whose fear is that the other world
Will end it. But I wait uneasy here
Under the creaking trees, the low dark sky,

For the conspirators. This is the place
Where I come, in better weather, with a book
Or pen and paper – for I must confess
To a little amateur scribbling. Love and letters:
One ought to be content – would, if the times
Were different; if state and man were free,
The slaves fed well, and wars hung over us
Not with death's certainty but with the odds
Merely of dying a not too painful death.
Yes, I have caught the times like a disease
Whose remedy is still experimental;
And felt the times as some enormous gaffe
I cannot forget. And now I am about
To cease being a fellow traveller, about
To select from several complex panaceas,
Like a shy man confronted with a box
Of chocolates, the plainest after all.
I am aware that in my conscious wish
To rid the empire of a tyrant there
Is something that will give me personal pleasure;
That usually one's father's death occurs
About the time one becomes oneself a father.
These subtleties are not, I think, important –
No more than that I shall become a traitor,
Technically, to my class, my friend, my country.
No, the important thing is to remove
Guilt from this orchard, which is why I have
Invited here those men of action with
Their simpler motives and their naked knives.
I hope my wife will walk out of the house
While I am in their compromising presence,
And know that what we built had no foundation
Other than luck and my false privileged rôle
In a society that I despised.
And then society itself, aghast,
Reeling against the statue, also will
Be shocked to think I had a secret passion.
Though passion is, of course, not quite the word:
I merely choose what history foretells.
The dawn comes moonlike now between the trees

And silhouettes some rather muffled figures.
It is embarrassing to find oneself
Involved in this clumsy masquerade. There still
Is time to send a servant with a message:
'Brutus is not at home': time to postpone
Relief and fear. Yet, plucking nervously
The pregnant twigs, I stay. Good morning, comrades.

AFTER THE DRAMA

DUKE: Bear him away. This villainy will be
Remembered only as a moral tale
To warn our children. Come, my delicate pair:
To bed. Your pleasure's long been waiting there.

The curtain falls, the Duke removes his whiskers,
And there is no controlling force to ensure
That wrong is punished, and that happiness
Discovers youth and beauty powerless.

In the wings the gaolers have unhanded Cano,
The lovers separate with indifference,
And no philosophy can dissipate
For the tired Duke the sordid cares that wait.

The blue sky is dismantled: the lights go out.
Actors and audience become congruent.
And in the freezing street the newsboys cry
The frightful art that all must live and die.

The play's rich ambiguities assume
A rule of conduct in the viewer's mind;
Its subtle music fades as soon as uttered.
Now the great portals of the place are shuttered,

And the playbills flap to nothing in the wind.
Has here, too, some wise ruler lent his power
To an ambitious devil that at last
Will face the formal gathering of his past;

And find prevented his high-sounding rapes,
His avarice unmasked he named the social
Order, and see what half he always feared –
The unconsidered man resume his beard?

NEWSTEAD ABBEY

Birds on the lake; a distant waterfall:
Surrounded by its lawns, a vandyke shawl
Of woods, against the washed-in sky of March,
The abbey with its broken wall and arch,
Its scoured and yellow look, has power still
To move.
            The Nottingham Corporation will
At the converted stable block provide
Postcards and teas, and in the house a guide.

Impossible to doubt that he foresaw
His dwelling's destiny, the social law
Which now ropes off his manuscripts and bed;
That pathos and joke were clearly in his head
When for the sentimental lookers-over
He reared the conspicuous monument to Rover,
Designed the too-heroic helmets for
His tripped-up entry in the Grecian war,
Made the monks' mortuary a swimming bath,
Loved these dim women.
               Lout, girl, polymath,
Stare at the puzzling relics of a life:
Grapplings with action, blind turning to a wife.

In bed he could gaze out across the scene
Where now the trees are heavy but not green
With spring, and see perhaps the rowing boat,
The little broad-beamed *Maid of Athens*, float
At her rope's end, past the blue toilet jug,
The tumbler of magnesia.
               And the bug
That impregnated then this habitation

And kept it quick despite the abdication
Of all it served, of that for which it was planned,
I know too well but really understand
No better than the guide.
                                        'The table that you see
Is where the poet Byron wrote his poetry'.

ONE AND MANY

Awake at five, I am surprised to see
Across the flocculent and winter dark
Windows already yellow; and am touched
By the unconscious solidarity
Of the industrious world of normal men
With art's insomnia and spleen,
As unaccountably as when
A long-dead negro plays through a machine.

I think of galleries lined with Renaissance man's
Discovery of physique, and jealously wonder
Why now it is impossible to show
Human existence in its natural stance –
The range of burgher, tart and emperor,
Set among withers, game, brocade,
Merely as themselves, not emblems for
A stringent world the artist never made.

Did the imagination then proceed
Quite naturally with a cast of men
Resembling the creator, who played out
Not anguish at the prospect of a deed
Ending a loathed society, nor that
Consideration shown by fear,
But were ambitious, usual, fat,
Pugnacious, comic, worldly, cavalier?

Not really so: the eye of art was cocked
Always from low and lonely vantages,
And the great boots and thighs, the glittering chests,
Taken for granted by their owners, blocked

A sky full of desired irrelevant stars
Whose enigmatic message lay
In wait until the rogues and czars
Fell ranting in a dynasty's decay.

And now art's only living figure broods
On the ensanguined falling moon until
The opposite horizon cracks and lights
Go out: over sapped and far-transported foods
I read of crises and prepare for living
In that strict hierarchy of
A miser body made for giving
And which prepares for war desiring love.

TO SHAKESPEARE

I turn your marvellous pages like
An invalid regarding birds,
Envying, too, your power to strike
Soft centres with a blow of words.

But more: within the words a myth
Resides that poets have to use –
Shamefacedly, as children with
Baths that their siblings first infuse.

And time removes from round the plot
Implausible or obvious coats.
I learn now, for example, what
Obsessional jealousy denotes

And think of all Leontes felt
Unknowing for Bohemia's king;
Why the short sword of Brutus dealt
A thrust at its beloved thing;

What made Cordelia dread to tell
Her love; and that compulsive feud
When the flat land of Denmark fell
Into a classic attitude.

No end to these great symbols of
The shapes that human life must take:
And moving from the sphere of love
I see the wider claims you stake.

The dynasties parade of weak
Crowns, strong usurpers, that agree
A course determined by the bleak
Impersonal force of history.

Fickle, emaciated mobs
Rage, and the common soldiers die;
By the rich coronation sobs
The fat rejected coward 'I'.

Your simple but mysterious life,
Its sexual ambiguities
Moving within a reign of strife,
Determined and experienced these –

Which now and till the end of our
Society and tongue will keep
Their verbal, archetypal power
To make the lonely Gellies weepe.

THE PERTURBATIONS OF URANUS

Such fame as I have drops from me in a flash
When the girl behind the café bar sends back
A candid gaze. I judge her by the lack
Of overt imperfections in her flesh
And by her youth, but fear she will advance
Such standards to me. I open my book and read
That the sole sin is human ignorance,
Through mind must stretch the future of the breed.

I agree, without reservations I agree;
But glance occasionally where the urn
Distorts the image of her whom I confirm
Is not distorted, and again I see

How still the world belongs to the obtuse
And passionate, and that the bosom's small
But noticeable curve subtends its tall
Explosions and orations of mad abuse.

A fraud, then, this concern about the fate
Of the supposedly less rational?
No, but the powers that dissuade from all
Libidinous action rise from our weakest part.
And I go out into the urban grey,
Where one vermilion bus sign hangs as though
Placed by a careful painter, and array
My lust with the armour of my self once more.

The planet Neptune's existence was revealed
Only by the perturbations of Uranus.
Crabbed lines of poetry, pigments congealed
Insanely on a little canvas train us
For those transcendent moments of existence
In which the will is powerless, and the blind
Astonished flesh forgets that it is kind
And drives in love or murder with its pistons.

Our art is the expression of desire,
Yeats said; and one who buys a landscape for
Its beauty takes home in his arms the bare
Outrageousness of an uncaring whore –
Among this trivial brick such rhetoric seems
Irrelevant to the short degraded lives
For whom the artist plans, the prophet dreams,
Perversely, virtuous law and golden hives.

Girl, through young generations still unborn
You will induce again and yet again
Disturbances within the learned men;
And they will feel brain from spare body torn,
Whether they hear, in ruins that their pity
Failed to prevent, their fear knew they would meet,
Or in the intact and reasonable city,
The disrespectful giggles of the street.

AMATEUR FILM-MAKING

A cold, still afternoon: mist gathered under
The distant black-lead avenues of branches;
Above our heads the drizzle ready to fall
Through greyness uniform, crepuscular;
And where we wander with the camera,
In the empty park, they have been felling trees
      And uprooting the stumps.

This is a portion of that film which proposes
To show the poet posed on various backgrounds,
Accompanied by his own voice, perhaps,
Reading a poem. The words will reinforce
The image only fortuitously, as
A crisis of one's life is impregnated
      With a cheap tune.

You say: 'This is ideal: I'll pan along
The horizontal trunks and you, near me,
Will be standing by the biggest of the roots.
The shot will end with you in close-up, leaning
Gently on your stick, expressionless, against
The complicated tendrils, stones, dried clay,
      Of the upturned root'.

The root is like a monstrous withered flower,
A Brobdingnagian mole or tumour, or
Some product of the microscopic eye
Of a romantic painter: and I stand
Beside it conscious, like a boy snapped with
His feared headmaster, of an incongruous
      And awful presence.

'I'm shooting now,' you say. 'Prepare your face.'
The camera purrs; you swivel slowly round,
Recording first the black recumbent forms,
Like shattered marbles, then the gasping root,
And finally I face the little eye –
Behind it yours, which watches in the glass
      The impersonal image.

'I'm holding this,' you say, and so I continue
To gaze, and decide it is impossible
Really to be expressionless. I feel
The initial cobwebs of the rain, and think
What jam I shall choose for tea, and of a book
I am reading on psychiatric art, and then
                              Of myself, the poet.

I suppose I must be grateful that I am
Unlike the vast world of the sane and mad –
Not ill enough, or too ill, to create.
The camera stops. 'We've got', you say, 'a great
Motion picture here'. 'You said it, dear boy', I say,
And demonstrate the indubitable rain
                              And that tea will be waiting.

POEM OUT OF CHARACTER

Rapidly moving from the end
To the middle of anthologies,
The poet starts to comprehend
The styles that never can be his.

The dreams of tremendous statements fade,
Inchoate still the passionate rhymes
Of men, the novel verse form made
To satirize and warn the times.

And yet at moments, as in sleep,
Beyond his book float images –
Those four great planets swathed in deep
Ammoniac and methane seas.

He walks the ruined autumn scene –
The trees a landscape painter's brown,
And through the foreground rags, serene
The faded sky, palladian town.

(191)

Or thinks of man, his single young,
The failure of the specialized,
Successful type; the curious, long
Years before earth was dramatized:

The West Wind Drift, that monstrous belt
Of sea below the planet's waist:
The twenty-one world cultures felt
Like fathers, doomed to be defaced.

Yes, these vast intimations rise
And still I merely find the words
For symbols of a comic size –
Ambiguous cats and sweets and birds.

Viewed through such tiny apertures
The age presents a leaf, a hair,
An inch of skin; while what enures,
In truth, behind the barrier,

Weltering in blood, enormous joys
Lighting their faces, is a frieze
Of giantesses, gods and boys;
And lions and inhuman trees.

SITTING FOR A PORTRAIT

To Raymond Mason

I

Committed to your impersonal scrutiny,
The searching eyes that look at mine unseeing,
I fear your verdict on my anatomy:
'There is a growth upon your inmost being.'

You work with that controlled, alarming haste,
As though an anaesthetic set a date.
I hear the pen's incisions, and my face
Tries to assume a calm, a mood, a fate.

Tries to assume what it has lost, in fact –
Identity: but now your strokes impart
That image to the paper; more an act,
I feel, of primitive magic than of art.

So this is what I am. Or rather what
I hoped I was – and wished that I was not.

II

Using as images my lineaments,
You have to make the poem come out right;
Attempting to arrange what life invents
In forms more meaningful, in better light.

Do you encounter stretched and clotted parts,
Or feel obliged to improvise, despair
Of reconciling textures with your arts,
Or long to end the quest before you're there?

Be comforted: it is not you who fail
But the intractable subject. I could wish
To have for you the satisfactory soul,
The certain shape, of apple or of dish.

Although I know you want to see, like me,
Always the human in reality.

AT A WARWICKSHIRE MANSION

Mad world, mad kings, mad composition – KING JOHN

Cycles of ulcers, insomnia, poetry –
Badges of office; wished, detested tensions.
Seeing the parsley-like autumnal trees
Unmoving in the mist, I long to be
The marvellous painter who with art could freeze

Their transitory look: the vast dissensions
Between the human and his world arise
And plead with me to sew the hurt with eyes.

Horn calls on ostinato strings: the birds
Sweep level out of the umbrageous wood.
The sun towards the unconsidered west
Floats red, enormous, still. For these the words
Come pat, but for society possessed
With frontal lobes for evil, rear for good,
They are incongruous as the poisoner's
Remorse or as anaemia in furs.

In the dank garden of the ugly house
A group of leaden statuary perspires;
Moss grows between the ideal rumps and paps
Cast by the dead Victorian; the mouse
Starves behind massive panels; paths relapse
Like moral principles; the surrounding shires
Darken beneath the bombers' crawling wings.
The terrible simplifiers jerk the strings.

But art is never innocent although
It dreams it may be; and the red in caves
Is left by cripples of the happy hunt.
Between the action and the song I know
Too well the sleight of hand which points the blunt,
Compresses, lies. The schizophrenic craves
Magic and mystery, the rest the sane
Reject: what force and audience remain?

The house is dark upon the darkening sky:
I note the blue for which I never shall
Find the equivalent. I have been acting
The poet's role for quite as long as I
Can, at a stretch, without it being exacting:
I must return to less ephemeral
Affairs – to those controlled by love and power;
Builders of realms, their tenants for an hour.

DIALOGUE OF THE POET AND HIS TALENT

Poet

I give you this calm, star-thick night of spring,
A hooting owl that freezes in mid-air
The foreleg of the cat; a garden where
You may make courteous contact, like a king,
With lower life; and in the house an earth
Of anxiety and love, with some escape
Through sleep into that country of your birth
Where the desire can summon up the shape.

Talent

And these could be enough: I want to use
That almost-face, those other worlds; the small
Existences that parody the tall;
The holy family, the dream's excuse.
But I demand from you an attitude –
What Burckhardt called the Archimedean point
Outside events, perhaps – in which the crude
World and my words would marry like a joint.

Poet

How well I know your wish! It is my own.
To be committed or to stand apart:
Either would heal the wound. Alas, my heart,
Too cowardly, too cold, is always blown
By gusts of revulsion from the self and aim
Of simple man, yet sharing in his fate
It cannot calmly watch the stupid game
With the moon's irony, the orbit's state.

Then I must be content with images:
At worst the eye's own coloured stars and worms,
At best all the reflective mind affirms;
Wishing to people steppe, metropolis
And littoral, yet only finding room
To note inadequately on my pages
The senseless cataclysms of their doom;
While coiled in others sleep new words, new ages.

THE FINAL PERIOD

I watch across the desk the slight
Shape of my daughter on the lawn.
With youth's desire my fingers write
And then contain an old man's yawn.

At first my only verb was 'give',
In middle age sought out a god:
Ugly and impotent I live
The myth of a final period.

I see within the tetrastich
A jealousy as gross, intense,
As ulcered that real love of which
Art's tragedies alone make sense.

He pulses still the man of force –
The armoured chest, the boar-thick yards;
And here the woman-nature, coarse
Beneath the dainty silks and fards.

Appalling that should still arise
All that is dead and was untrue,
That my imagination flies
Where now my flesh may not pursue.

Life goes on offering alarms
To be imprisoned in the cage
Of art. I must invent more charms
To still the girl's erotic rage:

Frozen in their betrothal kiss,
The innocent boy will never move
To loose the codpiece, and his miss
Stay spellbound in her father's love –

And yet the actual girl will sigh
And cross the garden with her flowers;
And I will leave the desk, and try
To live with ordinary powers.

Bermuda or Byzantium –
To some utopia of forgiving
And of acceptance I have come,
But still rebellious, still living.

The first absurd haphazard meeting
With one loved unrequitedly,
The insurrection caused by fleeting
Words of my own, while I stood by –

Those fatal and recorded times
Return like heartburn, and I see
Behind heroic plangent rhymes
Unutterable deficiency.

Even this noon of greens and blues;
June's badges, roses of human red;
Birds in the cavern of the yews;
A lark's quaver figure in my head;

The car in the lane that circumvents
The archipelagos of dung –
These trivial concomitants
Of feeling, these, too, must be sung.

And in the song all will be whole,
Immortal, though the author pass –
Ended his little speaking rôle –
On to the doomed and venal mass.

She comes whom I would marble through
Her painful and tumultuous years,
So she would wake at last in true
Epochs, to music of the spheres.

JAG AND HANGOVER

I have spent some days of late
Exalted, ambitious, free,
In a stupor of poetry,
And now I open my eyes
To find without much surprise
All incurably second-rate.

The muse's visitations
Fatigue and inflame the sense,
Are precisely as intense
For McGonagalls as for Donnes:
The word appears and stuns
The power to see true relations.

When we desire to say
'Red' and our pen puts down
'Cardinal' all the crown
Of our head becomes alive,
And we imagine five
Or six continents under our sway.

Our ordinary features
Harden to some gold mask;
Like the princess' task
Assumed by dwarfs, the long
History before the song
Can be lived by the singing creatures

Is over, and the earth
Has images for matter.
But soon realities spatter
Both lines and world with dead
Areas where the head
Perceives unsowable dearth.

And so our subject resumes
The massive poverty
From which, improbably,
Tribunes deduce the elate
Harmonious future state
Of rich individual blooms.

TO POSTERITY?

I wonder, putting down this opening line,
If what will follow's that unlikely freak –
The verse that must outlast my life and speak
To those unborn and send along their spine
The chill delicious hand that now I feel,
Truth in its ravishing mask of the ideal.

So that the composition need not show
The velvet nude or great empurpled sky
But merely what at present meets my eye:
The promising pen and paper in the glow
Of lamplight wars occasionally permit;
The books unburnt; the living flesh unhit.

This moment – reaching out towards the box
Of cigarettes, the brass-augmented theme
Announced upon the radio – is the dream
That I would wish to cheat the racing clocks,
Dials that mark the vital seventy years,
The culture's thousand, the coming lustrum's fears.

Though in such moment there of course will be
A sense of time undreamt of even by these:
Ages piled on the planet's flank that freeze
With inconceivable immobility;
And far back in the wastes the tiny span
Of the erect and big-brained Primate, man.

TO A FRIEND LEAVING FOR GREECE

From the Tin Islands' autumn where the foliage hangs
In green and yellow tatters like an old
Set on a provincial stage, you go
To burgundy seas, white harbours, empty skies –
Greece, with its islands like discovered bones,
Its names of our neuroses and its youth
Made dark 'with fabulous accounts and traditions'.

To disinter the universal crime
Of the legendary past is possible.
Possible, too, the survival of the once
Tormented and warring centre of the world
As fallen columns, terribly eroded
Decapitated bearded heads – ignored
By the quite happy and unimportant heirs.

You visit a country where the unclean being
Who brought disaster has already been expelled,
And far back in its history the gloomy date:
'Twenty-eighth year of the War. Blockade of Athens'.
Will you return with hopeful messages
For the new victims of the Theban king
And of the destroyers of democracy?

MYTHOLOGICAL SONNETS

TO MY SON

I

Far out, the voyagers clove the lovat sea
Which fizzed a little round its oily calms,
Straw sun and bleached planks swinging, the
Gunwale ribbed with a score of tawny arms.
Nursing a bellyache, a rope-rubbed hand
Or a vague passion for the cabin boy,
Accustomed to the rarity of land
And water's ennui, these found all their joy
In seeing the hyphens of archipelagos
Or a green snake of coast rise and fall back.
And little they imagined that in those
Inlets and groves, stretched out as on the rack,
Their girls were ground under the enormous thews
Of visiting gods, watched by staid munching ewes.

II

There actually stood the fabled riders,
Their faces, to be truthful, far from white;
Their tongue incomprehensible, their height
Negligible: in a word, complete outsiders.

Why had they come? To wonder at the tarts,
Trade smelly hides, gawp at the statuary,
Copy our straddling posture and our arts?
How right that we had not thought fit to flee!

'Join us at cocktails, bathing?' No reply.
'Let's see your wild dances, hear your simple airs.'
No move save the shifting of a shifty eye.

Trailing great pizzles, their dun stallions
Huddled against the hedges while our mares
Cavorted on the grass, black, yellow, bronze.

MYTHOLOGICAL SONNETS

III

The legendary woman he had sought,
Whose name had been as threadbare and remote
As God's, whose awful loveliness was taught
With participle, peak and asymptote,

Now lay below him smiling past his gaze;
The breasts a little flaccid on their cage
Of ribs, her belly's skin as speckled as
A flower's throat. She had been caught by age.

And he could see that even in the past
The pillars that enclosed the myth concealed
A slippery stinking altar and a vast
Horde of lewd priests to whom all was revealed.

Yet she was fair still, and he cried out in vain
To reach and own her far complacent fane.

IV

Beneath a bit of dirty cloth a girl's
Thin severed hand; a portrait of a man
Streaming with blood from badly painted curls;
A withered heart just pulsing in a pan.

Even though these have been displayed to us
Can we believe them or the cause of their
Existence, comically anomalous?
Here under peeling walls, a sceptic stare,

The hand writes its seditious words of love,
Belief goes on being painfully expressed,
And pity flutters at its far remove
From the historical tormented breast.

Did God intend this squalid spuriousness
To mean both what it is and purports? Yes.

A granulated, storm-blown, ashen sky
Behind blanched, still unruined columns where
Monarch and queen, prophetic sister, dry
Old statesman still descend the marble stair.

'You are my destiny.' 'Do not go forth
Today in combat.' 'This whole realm is sick.'
Their voices rise into the breaking light
And die away towards the barbarous north.

These could not, though half conscious of their plight,
Grasp the extent of time's appalling trick
That stole the flesh that was so sweet and thick,
Broke wall and bones, saved from the gorgeous site
Some kitchen pot, discarded and obese,
And gave the great names to horses and disease.

The sage cut an orange through the navel, dwelt
Upon the curious pattern then revealed.
Breaking a habit makes the world, he felt,
Burst out with meanings usually concealed.

Experimenting later with that girl
Who cooked his rice and dusted all his books,
He saw what he had never seen – a curl
Soft in the well where the neck's sinews rise,
And yearned in pity that with no rebuke
She lent herself to these perverted grips.

But as for her, she never thought her lot
Called for emotion. This strange exercise
Came with the rice and dust – the habitual cut
Of a world small and dry and full of pips.

VII

Well now, the virgin and the unicorn –
Although its point and details are obscure
The theme speeds up the pulses, to be sure.
No doubt it is the thought of that long horn
Inclined towards a lady young, well-born,
Unfearful, naïve, soft, ecstatic, pure.
How often, dreaming, have we found the cure
For our malaise, to tear or to be torn!

In fact, the beast and virgin merely sat,
I seem to think, in some enamelled field;
He milky, muscular, and she complete
In kirtle, bodice, wimple. Even that
Tame conjugation makes our eyeballs yield
Those gems we long to cast at someone's feet.

VIII

Suns in a skein, the uncut stones of night,
Calm planets rising, violet, golden, red –
Bear names evolved from man's enormous head
Of gods who govern battle, rivers, flight,
And goddesses of science and delight;
Arranged in the mortal shapes of those who bled
To found a dynasty or in great dread
Slept with their destiny, full-breasted, white.

But long before stout Venus, clanking Mars,
What appellations had the eternal stars?
When, cheek by jowl with burial pits, rank dens
Lay open to the dark, and dwarfish men
Stared under huge brow-ridges, wits awry,
What fearful monsters slouched about the sky?

IX

Naked, the girl repelled his lustful hands:
Her shining skin exuded awe, like art.

The visiting god held out his simple gift
And, stepping modestly across the sands,
The innocent fool played her predestined part
And clad herself in the lubricious shift.

Years later and from that same place their child,
Lugging his vessel to the sheltered reach,
Started on his heroic bloody fate.
The ancient motive of his father bent
His gaze towards the ocean, wine-dark, wild:
He never saw upon the trampled beach
The thing that had assumed, but all too late,
The hard epidermis of a succulent.

X

Girls fight like fiends in paintings to defend
Themselves from centaurs: envious, outraged,
We never think (our feelings too engaged)
The crisis through to its surprising end
When the sad, baffled beast with clumsy hooves
Paws impotently at the delicate
And now relenting limbs. So Hercules,
Whose lovely wife the centaur Nessus got,
Should not have loosed at him the angry shot
That stained the shirt that brought the hero's fate.

I do not know what this conclusion proves
Unless it is that honest lust will freeze
To piteous art, and subtle jealousy
Must poison needlessly what has to be.

XI

Mysterious indeed are epochs, dates
And influences: how a woman springs
Into a painting of organic things
And gradually moves forward till the great

Shoulders and flanks blot out the foliate
Sepia. Then once more the fashion swings:
Among a tempted saint's imaginings
A thin pot-bellied virgin emanates.

Even the most serene and opulent
Goddesses rise from the sordid life of man,
Who catching, say, a girl in stockinged feet
Arranging a shop window sees the event
Translated to a new and staggering span
Of art, the previous pantheon obsolete.

XII

That the dread happenings of myths reveal
Our minds' disorder is a commonplace.
Myths, too, are history's half-forgotten face
Remoulded by desire, though we will feel
Compared with myths contemporary life unreal.
Tower and wall may sink without a trace
But the strong sense of lust and of disgrace
Lives on.
                    Ourselves have seen Prometheus steal
The fire the overlords denied to man,
Which act enchained him to Caucasian rocks.
We still await the hero that must free
The great conception whose ambiguous plan
At once brought to the world its evil box
And the sole chance to share felicity.

XIII

Once brought indoors the leaf-eyed cat became
An emblem disproportionately odd.
Its blunt head, much enlarged but looking tame,
Displaced the human lineaments of God.
The teasing beast that squatted on her rock

(206)

And ate the duffers had a feline face,
And even he who turned the riddle's lock
Went on to symbolize mankind's disgrace.

Down corridors of night an awful thing
Brushes against us softly like a wing.
Our hands that reach across the bed for her
We love meet unexpected, frightening fur.
And looking in the glass we find at last
The claw-made lacerations of the past.

XIV

Discovered in this vine-ridged, rounded land
In which its tutelary goddess, tanned
And huge, had spent her slender mortal youth –
A number of ancient men. Old age, old age!
Wine, evening sunshine, philosophic truth –
Nothing can still that agonizing rage
For what was never ruled but for an hour
And now lies far beyond the sceptre's power.

Towards the temple stride young girls whose dress,
Taut with the zephyr of their passage, shows
The secret lack which men initially
Despise, then eye with tragic covetousness,
And lastly envy, conscious of the blows
Time hammers on their superfluity.

XV

Even (we think) the heroes cracked at last –
Great lumping extroverts with shields that pelts
Of only fabulous beasts could cover, vast
Lickerishness and canyons of half-healed welts.

The man of ordinary valour, size,
Finds it impossible to visualise

These others – who had been alone with girls
On islands, with their deeds like daydreams, curls,

Hawk profiles, iron paps – that these could creep
Far from the friendly tents, the invading hordes,
And throw themselves upon the ground and weep
Or, growing mad, attempt to eat their swords.

Such were the flaws their sires could not foresee,
Blinded by marvellous human nudity.

XVI

How startling to find the portraits of the gods
Resemble men! Even those parts where we
Might have expected to receive the odds
Are very modest, perhaps suspiciously.

For we cannot forget that these aloof and splendid
Figures with negligible yards and curls
Arranged in formal rising suns descended,
With raging lust, on our astonished girls –

No doubt because they were intimidated
By their own kind (those perfect forms that man,
Ironically, has always adulated)
And craved the extravagance of nature's plan.

So that humanity's irregular charms
In time fused with divine breasts, buttocks, arms.

XVII

We read of children taken by the heel
And tossed over battlements; a sharp hot stake
Sizzling in a giant's eye; and near a lake
Two tender virgins lying naked while
Unknown to them four indescribable

Monsters approach. That world, we much would like
To think, is simply an artistic fake,
Nothing to do with that in which we dwell.

But could mere images make even now
Ears drum with lust, the chest run secret shame?
The myths are here: it was our father's name
The maiden shrieked in horror as she turned
To wrinkled bark; our dearest flesh that burned,
Straddling her legs inside the wooden cow.

XVIII

The stench hung even in the garden: down
The corridor it thickened: in the room
It strangled us. The visage, cramped and brown,
Seemed to belong already in the tomb.

'How long has he been at this dreadful point?'
– Idle remark to try to hide our fears;
But the astonishing reply was: 'Years.'

And as the sheet was lifted to anoint
The noisome wound we shudderingly turned
And tried to understand what we had learned:

That this old squalid hurt was done some bright
Day when it seemed there was no end to truth,
And the large heroes wandered in the sight
Of gods still faithful, through the planet's youth.

XIX

Stone countenances, bearded, ill with time;
The screeching class of starlings, dissident,
In cultured cities; crooked wigs of lime
That contradict the famous masks' intent –
The nervous images that haunt an age
Bud in the unremembered past and flower

In that long battle art and history wage:
And epochs compressed in childhood and the womb
Breed the regalia of the public hour.
The murdered father's head leans by those doors;
The brothers' quarrel stands behind the doom
Of one life's sickening and recurrent wars;
And the smooth tongue that offers love is built
On teeth ground flat in violent dreams of guilt.

VII

VII

MONOLOGUE IN AUTUMN

With yellow teeth the hunter tears and crunches
Whole boughs of the quince, then walks away,
His hind legs on a mannequin's straight line.
The clipped back (ample as a bed, unyielding
Save for a slight threat like an anchored ship)
Returns what always astonishes – the warmth
Of a new embrace.

                   And you arrive. I help
To raise your body in its carapace
Of steel and leather. Then I see you move,
A centaur, down the slopes towards the plain
Where in the mist the sun already hangs
Its monstrous copper and autumnal shape.

You fade. I turn across the leaf-crumbed lawn:
Under the mulberry the gales have torn
A cat gnaws the purple lining of the pelt
It emptied yesterday.

                 And now the house:
First the twin balustrades and then the busts
Whose formal curls and noses are as rough
As if their existence truly were marine
Under the window's random lights. Inside,
The books propound what all books must propound:
Whether man shall accept the authority of God
Or of his senses.

                 In the drawing room
The fire sadly burns for no one: soon
Your guests will descend, taste tea on Sunday tongues;
Their lives and mine and yours go on with talk,
The disposition of chairs and lamps, the opened
Doors to the terrace, the order of good-nights.

Hard to imagine that the ambassador,
Your cousin, lives at this same hour among
Furs, fuming breaths, ardours of moral striving;
That such half world exists for which our own
Has manufactured all its cruel swords and faces
Whose profits surround us here as love affairs,

Portable sketching outfits, hair arranged
Like savages and scented with the whole
Resources of science.
                              Yet this must account
For what I feel, in love with you, within
This house and season – that residual sadness
After bare rooms and trees have been subtracted
And love has learned the trick of suffering
Its object's relative indifference.
Why, as you always ask, should I so dread
What threatens from the rivalry of two
Crude ways of life, two grotesque empires, whose
Ideals, diplomacy and soldiery
We must despise? But merely to formulate
The question seems to me to answer it,
And show that shameful collective death as quite
Other than what we think of in the dawn –
The torturer that will test us in our cell.

I open the piano, sound a note,
Remember dreams. How could you come to grow
In my imagination (that must have been
My wish) so sallow and in such a place –
As strange and circumstantial as the future?
You said the words too wild to be recalled,
Lay back and gently died.
                              You will return,
Your horse not sweating quite enough to mark
The lapse of time. I shall forbear to ask
The question that makes pain a certainty,
But merely look with the avoiding eyes
Of a Cesario or Cordelia.

And dinner will stretch into drowsiness,
Owls swing like theatre fairies past the moon
Whose battered lantern lights the tops of woods
And shines along the calm, dividing sea,
Painting with fire the armour in the harbours
Which lie encircled by their snowy lands
And multiplicity of helpless wills.

The uninvited images invade
The separate and sleeping heads: dead branches
Threading the sockets of those equine skulls
Whose riders perished in the useless war,
Whose teeth are rattled in their open jaws
By tempests from sastrugi, and whose foals
Stream through what whitens their brazil-nut eyes
Towards savannahs where the planet holds
Only inhuman species to its pap.

ON THE MOUNTAIN

I

Why red, why red? I ask myself, observing
A girl's enamelled nails, not understanding
The convention – an unrealistic art.

I live in a suburb of the capital,
A hill of villas, and sometimes note such things;
Old enough to remember better days.

The stoics have virtually disappeared.
I like to think myself the last of them,
Shaken but not devoured by ghastly omens.

The theatres are given up to leg shows
And gladiatorial games. The savage beasts
Are weary with the number of their victims.

In poetry the last trace of conviction
Has long since been extinguished. Round the temples
Are crowds of flautists, eunuchs and raving females.

The decoration of the baths and other
Edifices of importance is assigned
To those same careless slaves who mix the mortar.

The so-called educated classes share
The superstitions and amusements of
The vulgar, gawping at guts and moaning singers.

Atrocious taxes to 'defend' the frontiers;
Fixing maximum prices yet deploring the black market
– These the preoccupations of the state.

And the alarming aspect of imperial
Succession! The imperial madness! O
My country, how long shall we bear such things?

I find a little comfort in recalling
That complaints of evil times are found in every
Age which has left a literature behind:

And that the lyric is always capable
Of rejuvenation (as is the human heart),
Even in times of general wretchedness.

II

In my garden, at the risk of annoying my cat,
I rescue a fledgling: as it squeaks, I see
That its tongue is like something inside a watch.

They would not find it odd, those Others –
Mysterious community, not outside
And not within the borders of the empire;

Not the barbarians precisely nor
The slaves: indeed, from their strange treason no
Mind is exempt ... even the emperor's!

Could I believe? Surrender to the future,
The inevitability of the future – which
Nevertheless can only come by martyrdom?

Respect those priestly leaders, arguing
Whether the Second Person of the Three
Is equal or subordinate to the First?

While in their guarded monasteries they lift
Their greasy cassocks to ecstatic girls –
Under the bed their secret box of coin.

I suppose their creed must conquer in the end
Because it gives the simplest and most complete
Answer to all men ask in these bad years.

Is there a life beyond this life? Must art
Be the maidservant of morality?
And will the humble triumph? Yes. Yes. Yes.

Disgusting questions, horrible reply;
Deplorable the course of history:
And yet we cannot but regard with awe

The struggle of the locked and rival systems,
Involving the entire geography
Of the known world, through epochs staggeringly prolonged.

To name our cities after poets, or
To hasten the destruction of the species –
The debate continues chronic and unresolved.

III

How rapidly one's thoughts get out of hand!
With my unsatisfactory physique
I watch the blossom through the blinding rain,

Cringe the while at the shoddy workmanship
Of the piddling gutter – typical of the times –
And stroke with skeleton hand the mortal fur.

It is as hard to realize where we are
As for the climber on the famous peak
For whom the familiar outline is no more

The record of a deadly illness or
The tearing organs of a bird of prey
But merely boredom, breathing, prudence, stones.

FAUSTIAN SKETCHES

Faust and the Dancers

I saw their skirts' inverted petals
All frail and overblown,
Their heads of various shining metals,
Their arms that would have flown
Save for the dovetailed bone.

I saw the tights, chalk-white, unwrinkled,
Full of their fated shapes,
The dark or sparkling beasts' fur sprinkled
Down deeply-valleyed napes,
The breasts unround as grapes.

I wanted privately to whisper
Their fragile public name,
Become the tease, the pet, the lisper,
Transformer of their shame,
The partner in the game.

Sick of my years' renunciations,
Pretence of calm at joy
Bequeathed to following generations,
What soul would I destroy
To be again a boy!

Indeed, I deny that soul lives after
The power has gone to bend
These slanting spines beneath one's laughter
Till dancers all contend
Against the dance's end.

Faust Bathing

Standing with girded loins beside
Thalassa, watching in the tide
The bathers white as halibut,
There comes the feeling in the gut

For piteous humanity.
These faces, vulgar, gay, unfree,
These bums divided like a root,
These breasts impossible or cute,
And varied, as signatures, these howls
As from absurd displaying fowls,
Remind me of my superior brain,
My aptness for intenser pain,
And my paralysis before
That bleeding accident, the core
Of living.

               Now I plunge. The cold
Deludes me that I am not old.
The stringy limbs are galvanized
Like one of my own frogs, surprised
By current from the jars, and speed
Through foam, turds, condoms, bootlace weed.
Soon spent, I turn upon my back:
The billows nicely weigh the slack;
Above their syrup greens a slow
Sea-bird, brown smudged like urban snow,
Sails skies as soft as towelling.

On land again I feel that wing,
The symbol of creative power,
Hang rotting from my neck. The hour
Has come when all philosophies
That seek mysterious unities
Of number, element and force
In stuff of air, star, gold and horse,
And those utopias of rich
Gardener, exiled tsarevich
And moral poetry, are able
No longer to console the fable-
Seeking imagination of
The sensitive, the starved of love.
Now only magic can reverse
The impetus towards the worse
And halt the atom in its rage
To burn the world, bring on old age.

Magic

It's magic that has ravished me.
Study to magic, magic to desire,
And magic is to set me free.

Though haunted by the poetry
That shows the age its mask of ire,
It's magic that has ravished me.

I serve that plain philosophy
Whose world is merely air, earth, fire –
And magic is to set me free.

In impotent maturity
I see afresh love's lewd attire:
It's magic that has ravished me.

Power to transcend the sad toupée,
The miser heart, I shall require.
And magic is to set me free

To range the kingdoms of the sea
And pluck the salt rose from the briar.
It's magic that has ravished me
And magic is to set me free.

Dreams in the City

The luxury of cities prompts
Deluded dreams. Of accumulating
Intaglio rings depicting, say,
The sauromatic virgins or
A tiny priest with golden bough.
Of cornering the market in
Rhinocerous horn or yellow pepper.
Of being done in terre-verte
Or bronze by some heroic artist.
Of selling against the frightful future
Or buying against the certainty
Of the exploiters' immortality.

Fluently I write astounding words:
The force that bends missiles to the brain
Equals the wave that pulls maroon
And brown from the uncoloured moth;
And all this substance of the world
Was not created, yet lacked being
Before it flew away as stars.

Or: Faust abducted from her Duke
The grave clever beauty, starved of love.

In certain streets there seems to be
A scattering in the air – not starlings
Or dust or abandoned wrappings but
The very sordidness of the city,
Though here might stand the famous piles
I long to inhabit in the roles
That need a purple wig or huge
Cuirass with simulated paps.

But in dreams I feel myself at one
With my times and think it no disgrace
To share the lust for the principate;
And after all what great quintets
Were written for the viola-playing king!
Besides, the status quo can only
Be altered by devout ascetics
Independent of the enormously
Expensive life of cities,
Where under awnings metal ticks
On porcelain through the general sound
Of laughter, wheels and wheeling birds.
And yet how fresh the air in gardens
Whose boundaries heraldic cats
Conventionally signify,
And through whose trees there sometimes thread
Dead boughs whose canvas gently bears
Poppy and muskets to the heart!
Fresh on the skin, that envelope
Bulging with emotion, truly fresh,

So that with curiosity and passion
I watch the chalked and empty crescent
Fill slowly with golden light,
As though its meaning had been devised
By man – 'A good evening for verse
Or love or happiness or money' –
And not, as it is, an eye that sees
Even the disasters of its own
Order with complete indifference –
As: the collision of galaxies;
Life starting on primeval shores.

In the Wolf's Glen the seventh bullet
Killed a pale deer with flaxen hair.
The portents are sufficiently grisly,
No doubt, for all who sell their souls.

I hear a terrifying aria;
Flames send their giant shadows on
Tawdry and flimsy scenery.
Human ambition elevates
The humble, introspective self
To unimaginable cruces;
Where citizens actually see approach
The flat-nosed riders of the steppe.
Can I be that improbable
Singer, this the unlikely song?

Faust's Servant

I'm quite the opposite of my clever master.
He's at his books all day. I spy on ladies
And think of naught but filth, though there's no faster
Road for a chap to Hades.

I wish I had his brains to take my mind
Off of the feminine anatomy.
He reads at Greek and Latin till he's blind,
Doesn't see the things I see.

Today the girls seem bigger there than ever:
Not that I ask for anything so young.
It's just I find it hard that I shall never
Again slip home the bung.

A widow thirtyfive or so would do –
But what's the use of dreaming when my chin
Says to my nose 'How are you?' as I chew,
And buttocks are so thin.

When bladder gets me up at four I'd give
My soul for sweeter breath and tighter pills,
And sometimes for a second really live
With magic's miracles.

Jottings of Faust

I

Assuming spectacles enables me
Better to eye the pulchritude of girls;
But joy is dulled by realizing that they see
In turn an ageing man in spectacles.

II

Straight from my study's stupor I awoke;
Walked through the curtains to the dazzling sky;
Saw on a flower a frightening butterfly –
A long-horned devil in a battered cloak.

III

A thought occurs to me
As I comb my hair and see
The pistils at my crown
Of silver in the brown.

Not the familiar one
Of what the years have done;
Not terror nor regret
At all this coronet
Announces; but a quite
Impersonal sense of white
And coarse in common fate
With soft and chocolate –
Some creature of the snows
And mould that briskly goes
Before the aiming guns –
The sense of how life runs
In harness with another,
Its pale and powerful brother.

IV

The fountains only play
On Wednesday and Saturday,
But the momentary spray

Is caught by the camera
Of the lucky visitor,
Which also records the blur

Of Faust crossing the square,
To puzzle the developer:
'Who is the figure there,

That with ambiguous mission
Ruins the composition
Of the dolphins' ammunition

Against the sea nymph's arse?'
– A dweller in this farce
Of myth that will never pass.

V

That humans should engender ivory
Is Faust's, to him, surprising reverie
As magical day ends and through the dusk
Light gleams on Helen's even little tusk.

Helen

It staggers me to find between her thighs
The gold that struck me with such awe when first
I saw it like a halo round her head.

That I am kneeling here, that from her rise
The imperfections that make passion cursed,
That all the Grecian and the Trojan dead

Are dead indeed, that now I must despise
The breathing wish that from my old age burst
And stretched itself upon the crumpled bed,

That youth and lust are lies and are not lies,
That no man who's alive has met the worst —
These propositions fill my heart with dread,

Pressed though it is upon a breast whose guise
Was fashioned by a swan, himself immersed
In love profane, by human nymph misled.

Questions to Mephistopheles

I

'Why did I choose this trivial shape,' you ask —
'The rouge, the plumpness and the mincing gait?'
I answer: is it not appropriate
For one whose Master laid on him the task

Of undertaking that the Paphian flask
And the Circassian dancing girl await
The soul's vendor? Besides, one can't equate
The real me with any human mask.

I mean, think how God's hate must change the entire
Expression, serving Satan hump the back;
Imagine further how the holocaust
Of hell dries up the flesh, that devils lack,
Like angels, sex and therefore must perspire
In vile self-love. Perhaps imagine Faust.

II

'If Mephistopheles in serving Faust
Can bring on dancing girls and get him soused,
Why doesn't Mephistopheles thus serve
Himself?' It's not that I haven't got the nerve,
And obviously not because I think
There's any turpitude in sex and drink.

Why then? Remember that my former state
Was perfect innocence, without desire
Except to praise my God. Then came the dire
Notion He fell in love with to create
A being of moral cowardice and great
Pudenda. From that time His angel choir
– Thirst still unknown to them, groins still entire –
Were set to shaping man's disgusting fate.

Gretchen

He didn't talk of love at first,
But all he'd read and thought about.
A blackbird sang as though she'd burst,
And then the rosy sun went out.

It still was sultry in the garden,
And when at last he took my hand
I thought I'd have to ask his pardon
For sweating, burning, like a brand.

He told me I was innocent
And very beautiful and young,
But his best flattery wasn't meant –
Being the seriousness of his tongue.

He asked to kiss me. Oh I gave
My lips to him with all my heart.
Close to my ear I heard his grave
Voice vow that we should never part.

And when he gently went to lift
My breast, my only qualm at all
Was that he should regard my gift
As too ridiculously small.

This was not like those other cases
When boys have fumbled, brawny, red,
And I've stared at their indrawn faces
A puzzled breath before I fled.

Though as he slid beneath my skirt
My voice cried 'No' and 'No' once more
When staggeringly his hand begirt
What had been only mine before.

How could he like what I myself
Had, save for nature, quite ignored:
The part thrust on me by some elf
Forgotten at my christening board?

I'd put on new the drawers that fashion
Decreed that smart girls ought to wear.
They were not meant to rouse his passion
But to make ugliness lovely there.

He never saw their style or hue,
For with a surgeon's deft dispatch
He bent me to the pose he knew
Would let him make the outrageous scratch.

And in a moment all was done:
The pain, the dagger's bulk and range;
And the assassin looked upon
His murder's mess, emotion's change.

His love was gone: I said as much.
Again his hands sought out their goal.
He said: 'To have the right to touch
You there I've given up my soul.

'Perhaps it was precisely this
Was lacking as we closely fought.
I might have pressed a father's kiss
On one more guilty than she thought.

'And need not have exchanged for love
What lives on love's renunciation,
And shared with you the burden of
The cries of human tribulation.'

The Princes

A reckless use of fur and cloth of gold,
Wastage of peacocks, boars and apple fool,
Enormous men with hired tights and pig
Eyes who surround descending princes,
Bargaining at impossible hours amid
Small tipsy trebles and Mongolian
Acrobats – this is how fate is ordered through
The world's inhabited and cultured regions.

At such a weighty congress Faust arrives –
Another wizard (though a famous one)
Among decipherers and economists
And experts in the ailments of old men.

Having passed all his life through want and wars,
Innumerable wrong decisions, tyrannies,
And bluff field-marshals, he has always dreamed
Of finding a second youth and reckless power.

Two or three kings are playing in the garden
With variable skill at cup and ball.
'Peru, this is the celebrated Faust ...'
'How interesting to meet a real magician ...'
'Do you read palms or entrails?' 'What success
In the alchemic line?' The trumpet sounds.
All pass into the specially built hall
Which cost ten architects and many masons.

Platoons of pallid secretaries surround
Each place, at which are set the texts of long
Insulting speeches. The morning's business starts.
'Before we can permit our boiling oil
To cool we must be sure your catapults
Are pointing from our frontiers.' 'If your spies
Disguise themselves as dervishes, our kites
Will tumble fire-balls on your mausoleums.'

Faust makes himself invisible and gives
The Duke of Seville a buffet on the ear.
This potentate turns to his deadly foe, the Grand
Mufti, and dabs him with his withered arm
And overturns that paralytic Turk,
Whose allies, rushing for the door, collide
With the false friends of Spain. Thrombosis, rupture,
Incontinence of urine, rife in the hall!

Then Faust ignites some Chinese crackers, which
Explode among a group of experts in
Fearsome ballistics. They take flight. And soon
The gorgeous chariots and litters move
Along the dusty roadways of the world.
Faust is alone, and dares the planet's wars
To wound him more than his unease of soul,
Gazing upon the empty towers of man.

The lid is taken off the flames of hell,
An angel chorus opens in the sky,
Its fatal twelve the clock begins to tell,
Power and ambition see that they must die,
Irrelevant love is weeping where she fell
And Faust prepares to act the final lie.

Faust's life before the Change was all a lie:
To him the world about as bad as hell
Appeared, since he unduly feared its fell
Rulers, and he was quite prepared to die,
Could the affair be painless. In the sky
There was no father he might kiss and tell.

The only good, so far as he could tell,
Was to find pretty girls with whom to lie,
But him they saw as one about to die.
To have your thoughts on earth is perfect hell
When earth imagines that they're on the sky.
No wonder, tempted slightly, that he fell.

With profile, wealth and vigour, it befell
That his great moving moment was to tell
A simple girl that pie lurked in the sky.
And when this specious statement proved a lie
And he had left her to reside in hell,
He thought he'd find it easy just to die.

But see, the moment comes when he must die.
The pit appears in which the angels fell.
At last he truly grasps the idea of hell –
Despite his past, before he could not tell
Precisely how existence was a lie
Measured against the spite of earth and sky.

Is he by love, or something from the sky,
To be redeemed and never really die;
Or is the optimistic art a lie?

– Faust being right when in his grizzled fell,
Immured among his books, he used to tell
His fellow humans human life was hell.

Hell! a great legend spreads across the sky:
'Tell Faust he's dead but shall not ever die.'
Fell Gods sustained by weak men rarely lie.

THE HITTITES

Short, big-nosed men with nasty conical caps,
Occasionally leering but mostly glum,
Retroussé shoes and swords at oblong hips –

Or so the stone reliefs depicted them.
But how trustworthy can those pictures be?
Even in that remote millennium

The artist must have seen society
From some idiosyncratic vantage point.
Short, big-nosed, glum, no doubt, but cowardly,

For him, as always, the time was out of joint;
And his great patrons as they passed the stone
Would turn their eyes and mutter that complaint

Whose precise nature never will be known.

VERSIONS OF LOVE

'My love for you has faded' – thus the Bad
Quarto, the earliest text, whose midget page
Derived from the imperfect memories
Of red-nosed, small-part actors
Or the atrocious shorthand of the age.

However, the far superior Folio had
'My love for you was fated' – thus implying
Illicit passion, a tragic final act.

(231)

And this was printed from the poet's own
Foul papers, it was reckoned;
Supported by the reading of the Second
Quarto, which had those sombre words exact.

Such evidence was shaken when collation
Showed that the Folio copied slavishly
The literals of that supposedly
Independent Quarto. Thus one had to go
Back to the first text of all.

'My love for you has faded' – quite impossible.
Scholars produced at last the emendation:
'My love for you fast endured.'
Our author's ancient hand that must have been
Ambiguous and intellectual
Foxed the compositors of a certainty.
And so the critical editions gave
Love the sound status that she ought to have
In poetry so revered.

But this conjecture cannot quite destroy
The question of what the poet really wrote
In the glum middle reaches of his life:
Too sage, too bald, too fearful of fiasco
To hope beyond his wife,
Yet aching almost as promptly as a boy.

THREE BIRDS

Pigeon

A cropped, grey, too-small, bullet, Prussian head
Leading a body closely modelled on
A silly clay model for the sporting gun.

One shoos the other from the scattered bread,
Prolonging needlessly a marital
Irascibility. The bill could well

Support a pair of spectacles: instead,
All who will closely look at once espy
A geometrical and insane eye.

Abandoning looks to art like a diva, the young
Starling opens its bill at an obscene
Angle, and squawks.

Not art but wrath, no doubt, at seeing the wrong
World: felines sprawled across his green-
Crusted pie of worms.

Was it this bather-sleek and quartz-flecked rowdy
Who later lay upon his back and showed
That beneath his arms

The upholstery in fact was dun and downy:
Disdained except by one extended bored
Tea-sipper's claw?

Budgerigar

Head, miniature helmet
Of steel-white armour plate
To hide and facilitate
An apparatus for spying
Danger from every sense.
The eye, a camera lens
At its tiniest aperture
Whose bead of jet is closed
By an incredibly neat suture.
Mask, god of Nilotic lands;
Like an old semite, all nose,
With the beard tucked well beneath:

(233)

Twin nostril holes above,
Punctures of some dread syringe.
One's finger is clutched by the hands
Of a lilliputian orphan,
While on its agile hinge
The blunt tongue juggles with
Regurgitations of love.

ANATOMY OF THE POET

I

Mantled with hair, walled in with bone,
The skull breeds its terrific notions.
And then the little windows groan

Their shutters up to let the oceans
Gush through their tender apertures,
Blue shires round currents green as lotions;

Or black-pored mountains, gorse-egged moors;
Or rivers where weed trails like snot
On the white flanks of herbivores.

And thus the soul combines with what
It thought indifferent to its mad
Destiny, and with foolish hot

Optimism and in language bad
And gorgeous speaks to the object of
Its wish. The godly iliad;

The eighteenth attitude of love
Of second-rate Rachmaninov.

II

How liable to ulcerate,
The mouth where poems form! This hole
To succour and regurgitate,

This soft, sharp, empty, giving goal
Of other mouths – we utterly fail
To keep it for the vaporous soul.

What staggering words may we exhale
From rottenness; and even when
The structure like a lowered sail

Collapses on itself, yes even then
The orifice goes on reciting
Noble trochees, and seeks to fasten

Its sucker upon all inviting
Firmness, regardless of repulse.
But see the poet's actual writing –

No strings of lust or chancred hulls.
There all is sunlight, flower-decked bulls.

III

Some agile ancestor bequeathed
To the poet his poet's modern hand.
Round boughs coal-destined it was wreathed,

Or moved adroitly on the sand.
The limb that scribbles presupposes
A skinless and a suffering gland

Whose baby's great mouth never closes
Upon its speechless scream. To touch
The epidermis of white roses

With tentative love and then besmutch
Itself is what the hand requires,
Running blots into tears. How much

It longs to be the cook's or dyer's
Hand, whose deft motions demonstrate
A way of living with the fires

And hues of commonplace estate;
But this was not the sad claws' fate.

IV

And who decreed that it should be
Heart-shaped, the heart? And crimson, clenched
Around the strong machinery

Which warrants that the man is drenched
In blood from top to toe? And hard
If, as must be, the thing is wrenched

From where in happy disregard
It leans upon its beating side?
The seat of passion is this scarred

Muscle, but soon it may provide
Merely enough of that to keep
Its own gigantic needs supplied;

And sacrificial girls who creep
Naked, with naked steel, towards
The breathing breast will burrow deep

And find in the tangled mass of cords
No pulsing love but love's dead words.

V

It seems to concentrate the gaze –
A famous monument or flayed
Scar. Sometimes important: days

Of slogan, oratory, grenade.
At other times it shocks: the place
Where we were negligently made,

So crude as to call out for grace
Or pathos. And this dog-like trait
Is what engenders in the race

The power of spelling out the great
Unutterable aims of art.
For when we write about the fate

Of champions or of God's wide heart
What wells up in our throats and flows
Through our trembling pen is that strong part –

As though the angel and the rose,
Like love, must use the things most gross.

VI

A joke, the belly. Angels, possessing
No digestion, being fed on God's
Nutrient but deliquescent blessing

Model the serious life we clods
Should aim for, when, our paunches gone,
We must match up to periods

Of endless love and inspiration
Without a single belch or stab.
All that enwraps the skeleton

Suffers the canker and the scab,
And fears its change to pain and fust.
And when we contemplate the drab

Liver and wrinkled tripes, how must
We long to be entirely song
And dazzling feathers, or, like a bust,

All intellect and calm, its wrong
Cut off above where it might long.

MEREDITHIAN SONNETS

Incredulous, he stared at the amused
Official writing down his name among
Those whose request to suffer was refused.

W. H. AUDEN

I

To suffer, yes, but suffer and not create
The compensations that will cancel out
The thing: to crawl alone in the redoubt
Of suffering, like an animal – too late!
Even the ruined life deceives itself.
He looks in the glass: the handsome features show
Nothing of that foul spell cast long ago
By some malicious uninvited elf
Who ordered him to love a purple flower.
Even desire re-touches what it bares,
Removing all that's human – creases, hairs
And likelihood. A poet in a tower
With rapture watched an army dye the ford
And paper swans upon the stormy glooms:
Man's love is more primeval than a bloom's,
Another wrote, slain by a rose's sword.

II

Great suns, the streetlamps in the pinhead rain;
Surfaces gradually begin to shine;
Brunettes are silvered; taxis pass in line

On tyres that beat through moisture like a pain.
Doubtless upon such evenings some at least
Of those events that shaped his soul occurred:
Against the streaming glass a whispered word
Whitened and faded, and the shapeless beast
Drank from the dripping gutters through the night.
But all the child expressed and feared is long
Forgotten: only what went wholly wrong
Survives as this spectator of the flight
Of lovers through the square of weeping busts
To happiness, and of the lighted towers
Where mad designs are woven by the powers;
Of normal weather, ordinary lusts.

III

Rising as moisture in a cloven print,
Eventually it bears upon its bronze
A miscellaneous life of hulls and swans.
In puddles on the wharf reflections glint
Of leaning mariners almost on land,
And a red setting sun far out at sea.
Its purpose may have always been to flee
The bright temptations of the city: and
If man will follow, here he must embark.
And take the gulls in pennants to the deep,
And leave the gulls and journey through his sleep,
And sail into a harbour in the dark,
Wakening upon an unimagined scene
To strange confused remembrances, as though,
His wealth left to the poor, he were to go
With sensual body to a virgin queen.

IV

The worker columns ebb across the bridges,
Leaving the centre for the few ablaze.
In bars, fox terriers watch their masters raise
Glass to moustache; and rain streams from the ridges

Of blackened balustrades and capes of girls.
To death and rubbish theatres resound:
Dummies in shops imperfectly expound
The nude: throats raise the temperature of pearls.
Luxury and moderate gaiety disguise
The flight of coin, the absence of ideas.
Doomed certainly, he thinks, and feels the spears
Upon his flesh as he upturns his eyes
Towards the yellow face of time against
The racing sky. So this is the thing it is,
He says aloud, to live in mortal cities –
Haunted by trivial music, stomach tensed.

V

'You would not be surprised if I could show
Myself to you who thought that you were fated
Always to become one of the celebrated.
And yet with what amazement would you know
The man so different from his answered wish.'
Thus he addressed his childhood in the minutes
Of calm, when the unfrightened lamp within its
Cone holds the sleeping tablets, book, and dish
For ash, and still in unimportance stand
Mirror, mahogany and hanging shirt –
Fairy tale characters that squeak and hurt
At some clandestine hour. 'From your far land,
In fact, comes the pallid thing that in the night
Starts at its image and the glimmering shapes.
Concomitants of youth, the rumoured rapes
Of queens: what now is threatening my sight?'

VI

Mouths pallid mauve, eyes in mock sleepless rings –
However strange the style, the heart responds
To each new generation's browns and blondes
With chaste illegible imaginings.

Girls cluster at the corner of the street
With feathered heads of birds, on legs of birds:
Their high indifferent voices utter words
Whose spell the meaning cannot quite defeat.
Behind, in concrete neutral as a gull,
The slavish windows of the epoch stare,
But through those lips the corresponding air
Emerges with romance ineffable;
And he desires that what he sees will be
Uncovered by a future plough in tense,
Glittering and perfect terms – false evidence
Of fleeting fashion, of his lunacy.

VII

The autumn wind had sounded through the night,
But stepping in the garden after dawn
He sees the flowers round the wounded lawn
Like posters, all their valleys filled with light;
Considers that the season is no more
Fitted to hold the cardinals and mauves
Than mind what it had called up in the groves
Of moonbeams at the dreadful hour of four.
The world begins to turn towards the task
Of living, and those self-destructive vows
That coincide with distant gear and mouse
And others' sleep recede: a formal casque
Replaces ghastly head and serpent hair.
Barred by the antechamber's ceremonies,
Who guesses that within is one whose cries
Ask no reply because they do not dare?

VIII

Some figures representing history,
Myth, comedy and tragedy are making
An offering to another, who is taking
All calmly as his due. Undoubtedly

This happened at a period remote
From ours. But what *most* gives him the blues
Is that the group includes the comic muse.
How could he, with his constant pains to note
The deadly parallels of time, bring on
Louis the Fat, say; or, his mind obsessed
With kings who find close relatives undressed,
Dwell on some lucky, sheep-dunged simpleton?
And surely he stays unheeded and unknown
Because he cannot grasp that laughter came
Before the daughters spat the searing name
And the uncovering of the jester's bone.

IX

Is it the tongue enslaves him to the land?
Turning the pages of a dictionary,
He finds the snail serrates the strawberry.
On chocolate furrows birds like snowballs stand,
While horses scissor pieces of the skies;
The ploughman's lips are dreamt of in a garden
Where spheres and spheroids in the light unharden,
And shadows tremble in the shapes of eyes.
Under the birch, the peasants and the deer,
The hills run chalky fingers to the waves
Where blue bays lead into the gantried naves
And smoking spars of cities. Seasons here
Contend with brick and iron, yet in spring
Frost goes away on waggons with the coke,
And larks rise through disintegrating smoke
And see it is an island that they sing.

X

You are required to utter what is true
By gulping insane amounts of water: or
You are cast up upon a burning shore,
And there the sister whom you never knew

Cradles your head across her naked thighs.
Such things may run in secret through his head
While he bisects a piece of breakfast bread
Or drives his motor car with careful eyes.
He thinks: my life and thought – stupendously
Incongruous. And then he sees the fat,
Bogus entablatures and columns that
Enshrine the god, the law, the currency,
Which to break down will cost the death of some
– Perhaps the girl who, loping down the stair,
Recalls to him his frame of flesh and hair
That at the least must hurt by being numb.

XI

Returning, sees his footsteps dark as blood ...
The snow itself seems to illuminate
The sky, whose jaundice the branches separate
With Rouault lines. A night like this, one could
Imagine that one still was in the age
Of imagination, and that warriors massed
Upon the snow – their hairy bosoms vast
With romantic love – like printing on a page.
Oh then, a marble temple was of marble,
And soaring colonnades apparently
Supporting porticoes in verity
Supported them. How did we come to garble
The message to the hands of what they make?
Though no less cruel, evanescent, blind,
Our cheap, scarred times have bred the usurious mind
And substituted fresco for mosaic.

XII

Yes, the dun monsters that loom up and pass
Are the celebrated buildings that in youth
Held those great heretics who spoke the truth
Even when, half consumed, the fire was

Removed from under them: and in middle age
Sent out the pirates in their little ships
To rob the gold from realms that robbed the lips
And ears of negresses. And now the stage
Is come when no one knows the noble tune
Embedded in the dull, unplayed toccata.
How different from the captain and the martyr
Is he who walks, this rainy afternoon,
The streets of monuments deformed by time,
Stopping at photographs of girls with flowers
For nipples and with thighs beyond his powers,
Racking his memory for a useless rhyme.

XIII

He reads a poem in a railway carriage
But cannot keep his glance upon the tropes,
And asks himself what is it that he hopes:
Criminal contact, fatherhood or marriage?
The child's grey eyes and tiny, dirty nails;
Its other sex; its beauty, unflawed, slim;
Its unembarrassed consciousness of him –
In which, however, he completely fails
To make out any element except
A curiosity sublime: is this
A human commerce far beyond the kiss
Such as awakened goodness where it slept
Inside the hairy capsule, or invented
Incredible ideas of innocence –
Conception lacking flesh and prurience,
And orifices marvellously scented?

XIV

The princess took the baton in her hand –
So small a hand, the handful huge enough –
But the vile beast, instead of casting off
Its hideous pelt, pressed forward to the land

Where evil never longs to be transformed,
And good is raped in every filthy ditch.
– Completely changed for him the story which
In youth had caused his cockles to be warmed.
Then is it that the world can really come
To be in three short decades what it seems –
A place of utter hopelessness? Are dreams
Of justice wakened by uranium
Beyond recall, and is goodwill from men
Quite flayed by torturers? Or has a new
Young innocent the castle well in view,
Prepared to try to love the beast again?

XV

The chill of autumn on a summer date
Reminds him, up at dawn through nameless fears,
How, due to uneventful happy years,
Man seems to suffer a precocious fate.
His dreams were of the time that crept on feet
Of tortoises, when love meant jealousy:
He sees now what he once tried utterly
To own, caged in a customary sheet.
Why should he rise from that lascivious nest
His whole youth yearned to make and frolic in?
Not that he loves the less nor that his skin
Has ceased to be astonished by a breast;
Rather, he's come to recognize today
How right love was to struggle to be free,
And in the softness captured by his knee
To dread to find the seed of its decay.

XVI

The wife was in the bedroom: in the attic
The servant slept, her cheek still smeared with ashes.
Diaphanous, the bedroom's shifts and sashes:
Around the servant's body, unemphatic

Calico. Yet the evening found his feet
Creaking the attic stair. At first she thought
To hide the hard ebullient flesh he fought
To show, and left him straddling the narrow sheet
The master of her inwardness and tears.
But later nights she was already bare
When he ascended merely to declare
How wild the wind, his loneliness and fears.
Soon he was visiting no more that room,
Preferring to continue to make cower
Beneath its silk the form he lacked the power
To waken, and speak freely of his doom.

XVII

Stands upright close to tree trunk during day;
Avoids men; somewhat gregarious in long
Winters; shows great affection for its young;
Comparatively silent; startled cry,
Like a laugh. He reads at night about the owl,
And sees through the uncurtained window blue
Emptiness, with only the argent moon in view
And one branch and the humped and hairy fowl.
And shuts the book and passes through the house
To where a woman is already sleeping,
Mortality upon her almost weeping
Eyelids. The owl is said to bring a mouse
Each quarter of an hour to its nest.
What can he lay before her vanished brood?
He holds some time his upright attitude,
Then with a kind of laughter gets undressed.

XVIII

The grass looks like some old and tousled head,
Each blade outlined with frost. A single tear
Rolls down a sunken cheek. The sun is a smear
Of ochre on the ice, itself like lead.

Inside the wool the body shivers round
Its shivering skeleton. No doubt, he thinks,
Somewhere a jolly god in musquash clinks
A pot of ale, and thumps a panting hound,
That whitens with its breath a marrow bone.
Or out against the palace-sugaring snow
The queen whose gelid lips are death to know
Glides on extensive legs and tiny zone.
And trains with tall funnels steam on Europe's plain
Past groves of birch, a drypoint's black and white,
Taking the wife and lover to the quite
Fictional life of ecstasy and pain.

XIX

Slipping on peach blossom in their drunkenness,
The Chinese groped for brushes to indite
A last epistle to their friend. At night
They started awake and saw the empty dress
Thrown on a painted screen – itself depicting
Some bridge where civil servants say farewell
When leaving for the distant capital.
And in the sober morning, contradicting
The flood of tears, the poignant characters,
A little housemaid, hitherto unseen,
Carries the steaming tea towards the green
Willow that shades the customary chairs.
This gown is far from empty: should it climb
Idly beneath, one's hand will find twin boughs
That bear divided fruit, furred as a mouse,
As though the peach had come before its time.

XX

The largo fades and what must follow comes
In its rightful place. The pauses are observed.
The tune proceeds from tree and mineral curved
In throats and bellies, urged by the proper drums.

The visiting presences obey the rules:
Mopping and mowing, conjure forth his tears;
Reduce to snarling mottoes all his fears;
Pretending folly to amuse the fools.
These mathematics deal with golden fruit,
Wild the successive halvings of the string,
Commonplace objects tick, explode and ring
To underline the prince's hopeless suit.
He thinks of dotty questions that the sage
Employs to seek the meaning of the rose:
What solid does a pair of sides enclose?
The Turkish rondo in a classic age.

XXI

If galaxies are travelling away
Not quite so quickly as the light they send,
Earth's telescopes may fly around the bend
Of time and see the start of things some day.
He listens to the weather from the room,
And later is surprised to find the sky
Swept clear of clouds which now transfigured lie
Along the street, reflecting human doom.
For him these ursine, warrior lights possess
No other meaning than the stuff they are;
His task is not to beg the distant star
Out of its white majestic dust to bless
The small affairs that stab him to the heart,
But with blue weeping eyes discern the cause
And use his alphabet to state its laws,
Leaving the words to childish gods and art.